FOR THE LIFE OF THE FAMILY

FOR THE LIFE OF THE FAMILY

Family Life Action Groups;
Starting and Using FLAG in Your Church

John W. Yates, II

MOREHOUSE-BARLOW
Wilton, Connecticut

Copyright © 1986 by John W. Yates, II

All rights reserved. No part of this publication may be reproduced, stored in a retrieval system, or transmitted in any form or by any means, electronic, mechanical, photocopying, recording, or otherwise, without prior permission of the copyright owner.

Morehouse-Barlow Co., Inc.
78 Danbury Road
Wilton, Connecticut 06897

Library of Congress Cataloging-in-Publication Data

Yates, John W., 1946-
For the life of the family.

1. Church work with families. I. Title. II. Title: Family life action groups.
BV4438.Y37   1986   248.8′4   86-21739
ISBN 0-8192-1399-3

Printed in the United States of America

2 4 6 8 10 9 7 5 3 1

Dedication:

With the deepest love and
gratitude to the two people
who have taught me most
about family life:

Susan Alexander Yates
Sue Tucker Yates

Acknowledgments

I am especially grateful to Judy Thomsen, Beth Pascoe, Jean McComish and Beth Spring, whose help has been invaluable in the preparation of this book. Also the wisdom and teaching through the years of The Rev. Chuck Miller has been a seedbed from which many of these ideas have grown. I thank God for these dear partners in ministry.

The article "The New Fatherless" from which excerpts are taken in Chapter 15 is copyrighted © 1983 by The Boston Globe Newspaper/Washington Post Writers Group, and reprinted with permission.

For the material in Chapter 4, the author is grateful to Ann Landers and the News America Syndicate who kindly granted permission to quote.

Portions of an article "Mothers and Other Strangers" in Chapter 16 by Deborah Fallows is reprinted with permission from *The Washington Monthly,* © by THE WASHINGTON MONTHLY CO., 1711 Connecticut Avenue NW, Washington, D.C. 20009 (202) 462-0128.

Also in Chapter 16 material is quoted from an article by Gladys Hunt, "Reclaiming Motherhood for a Restless Culture" © CHRISTIANITY TODAY 1980 and used with their kind permission.

CONTENTS

Preface		ix
A Word to FLAG Leaders		xi
1.	Why Is It So Tough to Raise a Family in Our Town?	1
2.	A Chapter for Single Parents Only	4
3.	Three Priorities for Parenting	10
4.	Turning Points in a Marriage	19
5.	What Did You Expect?	29
6.	Valuing Our Differences	34
7.	Deepening the Love Relationship	38
8.	Learning to Be Together	42
9.	We Need a Shared Faith in God	48
10.	How Does a Child Grow?	52
11.	A Child's Faith and the Sacraments	64
12.	Family Times and Family Nights/Holidays and Holy Days	76
13.	How to Talk with Your Child	96
14.	The Question of Discipline	107
15.	A Word to Husbands and Fathers	117
16.	A Word to Mothers	123
Afterword:	Where Do We Go from Here?	133
Appendix A	Guidelines for Leaders of a FLAG Group	137
Appendix B	Divorce and Remarriage for the Christian	157
Appendix C	Further Reading and Resources	169

Preface

This book is for parents of young families—couples or single parents who want to strengthen their family relationships and create Christian homes. As a pastor with five children of my own and a busy congregation bursting with families, I long sought for a book that would not only help parents learn how to build Christian homes, but would also serve as a basis for discussion with other families sharing the same goals. There simply wasn't a book that seemed right for this kind of study and sharing group, so I attempted to write one. To my amazement, our people have loved this manual and use it in countless study groups—which we call FLAG groups.

The Family Life Action Group, FLAG, is a small group of parents meeting together weekly for a four- or five-month period, using this book to learn together more about the Christian home and how to build it. It is not essential that you be a part of such a group in order to profit from this book. However, its benefits will be greatly enhanced if you form your own FLAG group.

This FLAG concept has been a great-help to many people. We trust it will be so for you.

J.W.Y. II

The Falls Church
Falls Church, Virginia

A WORD TO FLAG LEADERS

In order to assure that your FLAG experience is as good as it can be, you need to devote time to laying the groundwork and to preparing for each event.

Please read the guidelines for Leaders (Appendix A) before taking any steps to organize your group. Then acquaint yourself with how the manual is organized. The most successful approach is to begin with an orientation meeting, then spend a day and perhaps a night together as a group of parents away from all the children. After these two initial experiences, the group should be ready to begin regular meetings.

Specific outlines are provided for the meetings to enhance discussion of the reading. At least twelve meetings are suggested and two all-day or overnight retreats. If the group meets on a weekly basis, which I strongly suggest, allowing for some holiday breaks, the FLAG experience should last about four months.

The manual is organized in such a way that group members read a chapter (or two) and complete the few at-home exercises prior to the meetings. Whoever is designated to lead a particular night's discussion must study the outline for the meeting given at the end of most chapters and then make his or her own specific plans, using the outline as a guide.

# FOR THE LIFE OF THE FAMILY

CHAPTER 1

Why Is It So Tough to Raise a Family in Our Town?

A *Washington Post Magazine* article in 1982 responded to that question with several observations about fast-paced life in our nation's capital:

> It was a chance encounter at the Lafayette School playground. No names were exchanged. But she looked about 27, a pretty serene young mother with straight blond hair held in place by a tortoise shell headband. As she pushed her two-year-old back and forth on a playground swing, her diamond ring—a flash of income level—winked in the sunlight. There was something brand-new about her, as if she were trying out marriage, family and Washington. She was.
>
> "We moved here two years ago," she volunteered. "Actually, we're from Chicago. I like Washington a lot. There's lots to do, like the museums. But it was my husband who really wanted to move here. He's with an oil company and very political. He likes to be at the center of things."
>
> This short precis could easily be the profile of countless couples who migrate to Washington. Ambitious, well-educated, and wired like switchboards in search of connections, they arrive clutching their "cum Laude" qualifications, hoping to do good, or at least well. But unless they arrive well-fortified, the same forces that attracted them to Washington can wind up blowing their families apart. If ambition, ego and the lust for power blow like trade winds over other cities, they blow at gale force over Washington. The family, struggling to withstand the gale, either grows tough or collapses.

"Cities have styles," said psychiatrist James Gordon, who practices in Northwest Washington and is an associate clinical psychiatrist at Georgetown University Medical School. "Here it's the political style that prevails—which is essentially to conceal. The whole idea is to *not* say what's on your mind.

"I've lived in four cities, New York, Boston, San Francisco, and Washington. But there is more pressure on parents in Washington than in any other place I've been. The pressure to please other people at work, to meet deadlines, to obscure your real feelings about what you're doing and to what uses it is being put. People are incredibly harassed at work. It takes so long to cool out that by the time you do, it's time for the kids to go to bed."

"Child neglect is an issue here," said Dr. David Scharff, a child psychiatrist who has a largely upper-middle class practice in Bethesda, as well as serving as an associate professor at the Uniformed Services University of the Health Sciences. "It's not that parents don't care, but they're stretched very thin."

If I could wave a wand over the city," said Scharff, "I would try to get the mothers of especially pre-school children to stay home." (Phyllis Theroux, "Why It's So Tough to Raise a Family in Washington," in *The Washington Post Magazine,* November 14, 1982.)

Those of us in the Washington D.C., area *do* live in the fast track. But this breathless pace and tendency toward overcommitment is no doubt characteristic of your community as well. We are hurried, from rising to bedtime, and our children are fast becoming hurried children too. If we don't stop, pull back and examine all of this, we may discover that our children are grown and gone.

Can you imagine walking up to an airline ticket counter and asking for a ticket to "anywhere"? Of course that's ridiculous, yet many of us are guilty of building our families without any specific objectives in mind. Too many families are like the sand dunes, where I used to play as a boy in North Carolina. They are formed by influence rather than purpose.

A sign in an office said, "In ten years, what will you wish you had done today? Do it now!" All of us need to begin thinking carefully about what we want for our home life and our children ten years from now. Business persons spend huge amounts of money planning the future courses of their companies. They ask, "Where do we want to be in the year 2000?" But most of these same people hardly ever spend so much as an hour thinking and talking about where they want their family to be in the year 2000.

I have never met a couple who planned to have a mediocre marriage and family life, but we might produce just that unless we are willing to ask ourselves some hard questions and begin to set some goals.

Redbook magazine asked 730 marriage counselors about the most common problems that are pulling couples apart in the 1980s. As a result of the survey, *Redbook* published a list of the ten most frequent marital problems and listed them in order of frequency. The number-one cause was a breakdown in communication, and second was "the loss of shared goals or interests."

Most of us are so preoccupied with self-fulfillment that we don't stop to ask of our mates, "What *are* our goals?" In your family discussion, you will be encouraged to do just that.

As an opener, take some time to think about the following questions, and then discuss them with your mate or even with your children.

1. Do we really understand what a Christian family is? What guidelines has God, the Author of the family, given to us? Are we willing to read and study to learn more?

2. Do I really want my children to follow Christ and be committed to his church? What sort of parental example am I giving? Are there some changes that need to be made?

3. What kind of a family do we want? Do we want to be "outdoorsy"? musical? culturally inclined? athletic? intellectual? What kind of mood do we want to characterize our home? Laughing? Friendly? Quiet? Peaceful? Secure? Spontaneous? What sorts of things will encourage this? How do we want our children to feel toward us? Toward one another? Loyal? Understanding? Respectful? Or simply for each to go his own way?

4. What do we consider to be our most important convictions? Which of these do we want to see developed in our children? What do I want to instill in my children that my parents instilled in me? What not?

5. Realizing that what my child thinks of me will determine how much of my value system he accepts, am I willing to spend the time with my child that is necessary to help him to know me and understand the things that I feel are important about life?

If we aim at nothing, that's exactly what we will achieve. If we set goals for ourselves and our families and work toward them, we still may not achieve them all, but we will come a lot closer than if we had continued drifting on through life.

CHAPTER 2

A Chapter for Single Parents Only

Your presence in this FLAG group is probably more important than you know—not only for you, but for the others in the group as well. Probably you have been through a divorce, perhaps, on the other hand, you lost your mate in another way. Whether you are a man or a woman, divorced or widowed, most of your problems are shared by millions of other single parents, but are not understood by most *married* couples.

As I write, one of every five households is managed by a single person, and that will probably soon increase to one in every three or four. Forty-five percent of all children born now will live with only one of their parents part of the time before they are eighteen. But still, most Christian couples don't know what challenges you face as a single parent. One of the things you will do for the others in your group is to help them become more sensitive to and sympathetic to single parents. This is a rather important part of the FLAG process; but for *you* it is of minor importance.

YOU NEED THIS GROUP

You need this group for other reasons. If you will give yourself to the others in an attitude of openness and trust, you will develop something you need enormously—adult Christian friends who care about you just because you are you.

Being a single parent is one of the most difficult tasks imaginable. Therefore, since you are attempting such an overwhelming job, you need the support and encouragement of others. But there is more to it than that.

A CHAPTER FOR SINGLE PARENTS ONLY

Your child (children) needs the friendship of these parents also. If you are the mother of a young boy, the men in your group can offer him something that you cannot—the friendship and example of a Christian man. God has promised to be a "father to the fatherless" (Psalm 68:5), and one of the most wonderful ways He will do it is through the men in the Body of Christ around you. Being friends with them will mean more to your child than we can estimate.

The tests and temptations you face are in some ways harder than those confronting others in the group. Many conscientious single parents are tempted to give themselves fully to only two commitments—their children and their vocation that enables them to financially *support* their children. Because the overwhelming burden of these two commitments weighs so heavily upon single parents, they often neglect the priorities that I describe in chapter three, especially a relationship with God and with close Christian friends.

If you have opened your heart in faith to Christ, then you are *not* a single person. You are wedded to the Lord in a way that means He shares in your life completely. You do not "parent alone" if He is in your life. But, if you do not take time to deepen your relationship with Him through regular prayer, worship and meditation upon His Word, then your relationship will be so shallow and superficial as to be negligible. Your FLAG group will help you to discipline yourself to take this sort of time out regularly.

It will also ensure that you are growing in the second area of priorities, which is our commitment to the Body of Christ around us. One of the major ways by which God helps, guides, teaches and strengthens us is through other members of His Body around us. This will hopefully be your experience in the FLAG group. The Lord has promised to "never leave or forsake you," and one of the most tangible proofs of this is through the friendship of fellow Christians.

You face great tests as a single parent. You will be tempted to despair, to run away, to feel sorry for yourself, and to hate yourself. You will doubt God's love, you will be overcome by a sense of personal inadequacy, and you will be tempted to hate your former mate (if you are divorced). At times you will be so tired that you will doubt if you can go on. But you *can* go on, and the others in the group will be an encouragement to you if you will let them.

Single parents *can* succeed with the help of God. Your task is not impossible. It is worth remembering that some of history's greatest men and women grew up in single-parent homes and were raised by courageous, dedicated parents. One example from the Bible is that of Joseph, the great grandson of Abraham.

JOSEPH

Joseph lived around 1500 BC (Moses didn't come until 300 years later. The Ten Commandments hadn't been given. King David wasn't born until hundreds of years later. The Jewish nation didn't even exist at this time except in this family, Joseph's family.) He was born in the "back side" of the Middle East—what today is Syria. By all rights he should never have been heard of. His father, Jacob, was a shepherd. His mother died when he was a little boy. He had no formal education; and yet, by the time Joseph was forty years old, he was the most important man in the nation of Egypt, second in power only to the pharaoh himself. His leadership ability, his incredible organizational and administrative skills, his brilliance and his spiritual perceptivity were known to all the people of his day. In addition to that, you will find no blemish in his character—no indication that Joseph ever failed God. Surely he wasn't perfect and he had his faults, but the maturity of this individual, even as a boy, was remarkable.

What was it in his early years that enabled this boy to achieve greatness, not only in the eyes of men but in the eyes of God? You'll have to go back to Chapter 28 of Genesis and begin reading to understand all the intricacies and family relationships—the comings and goings that are background to the young life of Joseph. I recommend that you study the life of this son of a single parent.

His father, Jacob, whose name God later changed to Israel, had run away from home as a young man after cheating his twin brother, Esau, of his birthright and his father's last blessing. Jacob had traveled to the tent of Laban, a distant relative, and had fallen in love with the youngest daughter, Rachel. In order to marry Rachel, he agreed to work seven years without pay for his cousin Laban. Now Laban, who was something of a rascal, tricked Jacob into unknowingly marrying his other daughter, Leah, who was not so attractive. Then he said he'd give Rachel to Jacob only if he agreed to work another seven long years without pay.

In those days it was not unusual for a man to have more than one wife, but there was some jealousy between these two sisters. This was heightened by the fact that Leah had many children, while Rachel, the woman Jacob loved, could not seem to have children. For at least seven years, Rachel was barren, and it seemed Leah was having a child every year on schedule.

When Joseph was finally born to Rachel, it almost broke her already frail health; and it only increased all the jealous tension in this home in which this little boy grew. When Joseph was still a youngster, his father deceived his father-in-law and fled with his family and his possessions toward his homeland. During that long journey there must have been several different scars that were implanted upon young Joseph's personality as a young boy.

Psychologists tell us that events during a child's earliest years shape that child's personality for the rest of his life. If ever a young child experienced trauma, it was this little boy Joseph. For months his family was involved in a headlong flight across the wilderness, running away from an enraged father-in-law, running back to a possibly still-enraged twin brother, Esau. They had no safe place to call home, and during this time Joseph's beautiful mother died. Throughout this period, his ten older half-brothers shunned him, wanting nothing to do with this boy who was his father's favorite. Then his older sister, Diana, was raped; and, as if that were not tragedy enough, his older brothers brought unspeakable shame upon the whole family when they attacked, pillaged and murdered all the inhabitants of the city from which the attacker of Diana had come. The list of awful events in Joseph's boyhood just goes on and on. It's safe to say that circumstances were against his ever amounting to anything other than an insecure, frightened, bullied and, at times, spoiled young man. Yet, by God's grace and through his relationship with his father, Jacob, Joseph became a great man of God.

Perhaps you have had unfortunate experiences in your youth. Perhaps you have been mistreated, misunderstood, left, unfairly treated, molested. Perhaps you are still struggling to this very day to overcome the scars that marked your younger days. I want to encourage you, just as God enabled Joseph to overcome all these disadvantages, so He can help you and your child as well.

In Joseph's case, it was his father who played the key role in his healing and his maturing. Jacob was far from perfect. He was sometimes deceitful, self-willed, partial and cunning. He was at times a man of fierce, burning anger and at other times a coward. But he loved his son, Joseph, and that love expressed itself in three clear ways. This single parent's love shaped Joseph's character by devotion, discipline and direction.

DEVOTION, DISCIPLINE, DIRECTION

First, Joseph's father was devoted to his little boy. He cared deeply about his son and expressed it tangibly through gifts (like the coat of many colors). But, more importantly, he expressed his devotion in conversation with this child. In this brief section of the Book of Genesis are recorded no less than seven different conversations between father and son. If you are devoted to your children, don't just give them gifts—coats of many colors; give them your time, sit with them and talk with them. Make time for easy, natural conversation with them.

A good visit with a child is not something you can plan out ahead, but you can organize your schedule in such a way that you are with him regularly. Devotion to a child shows itself primarily in the attention and time you are willing and able to spend with him. But these alone are not enough.

Devotion without discipline becomes sentimentality. Jacob was not only a loving and devoted father, but also a strict disciplinarian. Any shepherd who lived out in the desert understood the vital necessity of personal discipline if he wanted to succeed. Although the Bible only gives us a few brief verses about Joseph's childhood days, included not by accident certainly, is a description of father disciplining son.

Our generation, one of the most undisciplined to ever appear in American history, has grown up in a time of peace and plenty and has been indulged by parents more than any other generation in our nation's history. As a result, the typical middle-aged, middle-class American is an undisciplined person. He can't stay out of debt. He can't keep his marriage together. He indulges his own personal wants to the extreme. He gives in to temptation and he regularly disobeys God.

Single parents, you must discipline your children. If they do not obey their earthly mothers and fathers, how will they ever obey their heavenly Father? If they do not learn personal discipline, responsibility and thrift as children, how will they ever learn it? Believe me, I know that children can wear you down; and the best-intentioned disciplinarian can fail. A child comes and says, "Can I have some candy?" And, after the tenth time of being asked the question and of saying "no," on the eleventh time, you throw the box of candy at him, saying "Eat the whole thing!" But, don't give up. Discipline your children. Do it with love. Do it with fairness. And do it with consistency, because inconsistent discipline may be worse than no discipline at all (more on this later).

The final legacy Jacob left his son was a sense of direction in life. We've noted that Jacob was not always the most imitable of men, but there's one conviction that grew deeper and deeper in his life, and that was that he would serve and follow and know the Lord. Maybe Jacob didn't know God very well; he had no Bible, no Ten Commandments, he had no instruction about worship, no parables, no Sermon on the Mount. Jesus didn't come until fifteen hundred years later. But Jacob had a deep faith in God, and, above all, he wanted to be faithful to God. That was the direction of his life. That can be the direction of any man or woman's life, however knowledgeable he or she is about God.

It hadn't always been so in Jacob's life. Jacob had not always wanted to be a man of God. God had blessed him with safety, with success all his life, and Jacob had always believed in God. But Jacob had to endure some sorrow, he had to wrestle with God before he really committed himself to the Lord's being King in his life. By the time Joseph was a boy, his father had settled the question. He had committed himself in faithfulness to God at all costs, and that direction wasn't lost on his son. In fact, it carried Joseph all his life through incredible hardships.

How can a parent cast direction onto his child? You do it by what you are. If you truly desire to follow the Lord, then your child will see it. It will be obvious. And yet, how much better it is to talk with him about God, to answer his questions, to read the Bible, to pray with him! Talk with your child of the things of God, of what it costs to be a man or woman of God and why it is worth it.

We will discuss these things in great detail in later chapters. Sometimes, as a single parent, you may feel uncomfortable, alone or inadequate. Don't cave in to these feelings. Acknowledge them and then ask God to give you anew and afresh, the sense of assurance, that even though you don't have a mate, you have Him, and for now, He and His people around you are all you need.

CHAPTER 3

Three Priorities for Parenting

Before we begin to focus too much attention on our children and our duties towards them, it's important to stand back and ask the question, "As *the* first parent, what priorities does my Father in heaven desire me to live by as a parent to my own children?"

Because He loves us as only the perfect Father can love us, God desires above all that we know and love Him. In his book *Knowing God,* Anglican theologian J.I. Packer makes the following statement:[1]

> What were we made for? To know God. What aim should we set ourselves in life? To know God. What is the "eternal life" that Jesus gives? Knowledge of God. "This is life eternal, that they might know thee, the only true God, and Jesus Christ, whom thou hast sent" (John 17:3). What is the best thing in life, bringing more joy, delight and contentment than anything else? Knowledge of God. "Thus saith the Lord, Let not the wise man glory in his wisdom, let not the mighty man glory in his might, let not the rich man glory in his riches; but let him that glorieth glory in this, that he understandeth and knoweth me" (Jer. 9:23 ff.). What, of all the states God ever sees man in, gives Him most pleasure? Knowledge of Himself. "I desire . . . the knowledge of God more than burnt offerings," says God (Hosea 6:6).

A Christian's first and foremost priority is his own relationship with God—Father, Son and Holy Spirit. God is looking for a growing love and commitment from His children. When questioners asked Jesus what was the foremost commandment, His answer was clear: "Love the Lord your

God with all your heart, soul, mind and strength." When the crowds came and asked Him, "What shall we do that we may work the works of God?" Jesus replied, "This is the work of God that you believe in Him whom He has sent" (John 6:29).

In the Sermon on the Mount, the Lord again stressed that the number-one priority is to know and love God. "Seek ye first the kingdom of God and His righteousness, and all these things shall be added unto you." To seek first the kingdom of God means simply to seek to let God be King in your life. This is illustrated in the following outline:

SOME QUALITIES WHICH ARE OFTEN PRESENT:

I. WHEN I AM KING IN MY LIFE

self-centeredness	anxiety
anger	apathy
discouragement	aimlessness
critical spirit	poor prayer life

security in things or people
lack of active concern for others
little sense of love for God
lack of faith

II. WHEN CHRIST IS KING IN MY LIFE

peace	purpose
joy	sense of security
humility	trusting in God

actively caring for others
a sense that God is using me
not perfect but maturing in Christ
deep desire to obey Christ
prayer life is real
learning from Scripture

To get from I to II involves, *first* of all, a change of heart: I must believe that Christ is the Son of God and desire to know Him better; I acknowledge my failure to be all God would have me be, and ask forgiveness. I ask Christ to be at the center of my life and to guide me and help me become the person He wants me to be.

Second, we don't change completely overnight. The degree to which these new qualities (II) are experienced in one's life depends on the extent to which one is willing to *trust* God and on the number of years that one has been seeking to let Christ be one's King.

Once we make the decision to ask Christ to be King in our lives, then begins an ongoing relationship. Our Lord has called us to be His friend and we cannot ignore Him. The whole of Scripture teaches us that God desires our prayers, our worship and our attention through the study of His Holy Word. If the President of the United States were to invite us to spend time with him, we would be quick to respond. How much more shall we seek to make a top priority of setting aside daily time to be with Him in quiet times of prayer and meditation on His Word. Probably the most important activity we can carry out on behalf of our children is to *pray* for them. Let me urge you to keep that list you compiled of qualities you want to pass on to your children, in a place where you will often be reminded by it to pray for your children that they will develop these qualities.

Second only to the love of God comes Jesus' teaching to love our neighbors. We know that our neighbor is anyone whom we encounter, but as members of a family, our first and foremost neighbors are those in our own households. That we should love our mates and children second only to God comes as no surprise, but, in this child-oriented age, it may be a surprise to learn that the relationship with mate takes precedence over that with our children.

God's desire for the husband/wife relationship is nowhere expressed more beautifully than in Genesis 2:18—25.

> Then the Lord God said, "It is not good for the man to be alone; I will make him a helper suitable for him." And out of the ground the Lord God formed every beast of the field and every bird of the sky, and brought them to the man to see what he would call them; and whatever the man called a living creature that was its name. And the man gave names to all the cattle, and to the birds of the sky, and to every beast of the field, but for Adam there was not found a helper suitable for him. So the Lord God caused a deep sleep to fall upon the man, and he slept; then He took one of his ribs, and closed up the flesh at that place. And the Lord God

fashioned into a woman the rib which He had taken from the man, and brought her to the man. And the man said, "This is now bone of my bones, and flesh of my flesh; she shall be called Woman, because she was taken out of Man." For this cause a man shall leave his father and his mother, and shall cleave to his wife; and they shall become one flesh. And the man and his wife were both naked and were not ashamed.

It was not good that man be alone. None of the other creatures could satisfy the longing for companionship, and God therefore created a companion for man to be a perfectly corresponding partner—his complement in every way. The King James Version says she was to be a helpmate "fit" for him (not to give him fits but to be the ideal companion). The old rabbis taught that woman was made from the side of man to emphasize that she was to always be beside him, facing all life could offer together as friends.

"And God created man in His own image . . . male and female He created them." Equal in every way—partners. Later God gave them children but not until they had come to deep commitment to one another. God never meant for our children to come between us and our mates. We are alone together as man and wife first, then children come, and then we are alone together again. We must learn as married couples to see our helpers/mates as our most important earthly friends and strengthen that relationship so it will remain strong always. Children will come and children will go, but the husband and wife remain. I am quite aware that in 1981 there were 11 million divorces and that one out of every two marriages ends in divorce, but this is not as God desires, nor does it have to be this way.

This relationship with our mates has four aspects—romantic, intellectual, emotional and spiritual. In the next chapters, we will elaborate on these four elements of the marriage relationship, but for the moment, please note what Dr. Alfred A. Nesser of Emory University School of Medicine has said:

> Parent-child relationships have been stressed so strongly for several decades that, for the sake of the child, husband-wife priorities are many times laid aside too easily. After the first child comes, a real test takes place. Will the mother now rob her husband of time and love for the sake of the child and ruin relationships there or will she continue to put priority on husband-wife relationships?
>
> It is good to recall that marriage is permanent while parenthood is passing. Since marriage begins and ends with two, the primary concern is to keep that relationship in the best possible repair. Then the child relationship will take care of itself rather well.

> Nothing is so central for a child's happiness and sense of worth as the love of father and mother for each other. There is no better way of giving the child a sense of significance than to see and to feel the closeness and commitment mother and father have.
>
> So parents should spend more time and effort in developing their own personalities and relationships. If father and mother are happy with each other, that contentment is conveyed to the child and results not only in good behavior and affection, but also in a sense of personal worth. Children are not meant to be the center of the family. That center is the relationship of husband and wife. (Christian Education Trends Newsletter; September 10, 1976.)

The third priority then *is* that of our children. God desire us to have a deepening relationship with them as they mature.

"You shall teach them [God's words] to your sons, talking of them when you sit in your house, and when you walk along the road and when you lie down and when you rise up" (Deut. 11:19).

Communication with our children is crucial. A famous and shocking study some years ago found that the average executive father in America spends a grand total of about seventeen seconds a day in meaningful conversation with his child.

The other day, my wife had expended her last available ounce of energy in dressing and seatbuckling into the car our twin daughters who had been unusually difficult that morning. She knew that if she said another word to either of them, she would regret what she said. They are nearly always perpetually in motion and chattering away at 78 rpm, but this morning they were exceptionally garrulous. After asking the same question four times and not getting a response, Libby finally said with a huge sigh, "Oh, Mommy, can't you speak?"

There are certainly these sorts of times when we simply can't communicate any more, but gentle and thoughtful visits with our children are essential if we are to follow St. Paul's advice: "Parents, don't irritate (exasperate) your children or they will become discouraged" (Col. 3:21).

> Love the Lord.
> Love your mate.
> Love your child.

These three goals stand out above all others for Christian parents. We cannot pursue any of them effectively unless our schedule week in and week out reflects consistent periods of time spent with each of these persons. Why not look over your calendar of the last week and reflect on the last few days. When have you been alone in prayer or meditation upon God's Word? When have you and your mate just sat and talked? When have you been with your child doing what the *child* wanted to do?

Living out these priorities, for most of us, is quite difficult, but not impossible. If this is God's desire for us, then certainly He can help us accomplish what He desires.

As if in support of these ideas, the following report recently appeared:

> Since most studies of family life focus on problems, Nick Stinnett, chairman of the human development and family department at the University of Nebraska-Lincoln, decided to give the flip side equal time. Stinnett conducted a national survey of "strong" families, and here are the six common strengths he identified:
>
> 1. Appreciation. Family members gave one another compliments and psychic strokes. They tried to make the others feel appreciated and good about themselves.
>
> 2. Ability to deal with crises in a positive manner. They had the ability to take a bad situation, see something positive in it and focus on that. They became a mutual-support system, and often rediscovered what they meant to each other.
>
> 3. Time together. In all areas of their lives—meals, work, recreation—they structured their schedules to spend time together. Many participated in outdoor activities—camping, walking, birdwatching—where there are fewer distractions and a greater chance to concentrate on one another.
>
> 4. High degree of commitment. Families promoted each person's happiness and welfare; they invested time and energy in one another and made the family their number 1 priority.
>
> 5. Good communication patterns. These families spent time talking with one another. They also listened well, which shows respect. They fought, but got conflict out in the open to talk it out.
>
> 6. High degree of religious orientation. Not all belonged to an organized church, but they considered themselves highly religious. The commitment to a spiritual life-style seemed to make them less petty, more forgiving, patient and positive. (Rekers, George: *Family Building;* Regal Books, 1985; pp. 35-50.)

AT-HOME EXERCISE

Before your meeting choose one of the following three passages of Scripture to study using what is known as the PPROAPT method, taken from the discipleship material of Barnabas, Inc. (P.O. Box 2012, Redlands, CA 92373).

PPROAPT

Pray initially giving this time to God and asking Him to speak to you through His Word.

Preview the whole passage. Look over all of the chapter briefly noting the context, reading the introduction to the book if your Bible has one.

Read several times the verse selected for study. You might look up the verse in other translations and copy these other versions in the left-hand column.

Observe. What do you think the author was intending in these words? Was there some specific situation about which he was particularly concerned?

Apply. Now begin to jot down all the ways you can possibly imagine that this passage applies to you and your own family life.

Pray. Talk to God about these various applications asking Him to help you put into practice what you have learned.

Tell the others in your group what you learned from this study.

Each passage focuses on one of the three priorities we've been discussing.

PPROAPT—JOHN 15:1–10

John 15:5

Verse	Observation	Application
I am the vine, you are the branches; he who abides in Me, and I in him, he bears much fruit; for apart from Me you can do nothing.		

THREE PRIORITIES FOR PARENTING   17

PPROAPT—I TIMOTHY 5:1–8

I Timothy 5:8

Verse	*Observation*	*Application*
But if any one does not provide for his own, and especially for those of his household, he has denied the faith, and is worse than an unbeliever.		

PPROAPT—MATTHEW 28:16–20

Matthew 28:19–20

Verse	*Observation*	*Application*
Go therefore and make disciples of all the nations, baptizing them in the name of the Father and the Son and the Holy Spirit, teaching them to observe all that I commanded you; and lo, I am with you always, even to the end of the age.		

MEETING AND DISCUSSION

After discussing this chapter, look at each of the PPROAPT Bible passages in light of the three priorities, keeping in mind the following questions:

1. What does the passage mean?

2. What are some of the ways it applies to you personally?

3. Which of the three priorities do you find you are having most difficulty with presently?

4. What is a specific area of concern, in light of all this, for which we can be praying for you?

Take some time for one or more persons in the group to bring others' concerns to God in prayer.

CHAPTER 4

Turning Points in a Marriage

That famous columnist on marriage and family life, Ann Landers, conducted a survey some time back in which she asked the question, "If you had it all to do over again, would you marry the same person?" (see *Family Circle Magazine,* July 26, 1977). Seventy percent responded, "No!" There were some invaluable quotes among the variety of letters she received.

> Most respondents were very candid about telling why they voted the way they did. One wife from Corning, NY, wrote: "Carl is one of those non-talkers you get so many complaints about. The last time he spoke a full sentence to me was Friday. He said, 'Pass the salt.' But actions speak louder than words, Ann. Today he brought home a dozen roses. I'm voting YES."
>
> From Davenport, Iowa, I received a curious card with two votes—his and hers. She wrote: "I'm a female, married 27 years. We are the happiest couple in town. I vote a great big YES." At the bottom of the card, hastily scrawled in pencil, was a word from her husband, who apparently had been asked to drop the card in the mailbox. He added: "That's what *she* thinks. I vote NO."
>
> One hundred and ninety women voted "HELL NO." One hundred and four men voted "HELL NO." Most of the "HELL NO's" were in extra-large block letters, heavily underlined and often followed by several exclamation points.
>
> A wife from a fashionable New Jersey suburb . . . wrote, "When we were poor, our marriage was fun. Things changed when my

husband started to make big money. We joined the country club, played golf and bridge. Then came the fancy clothes and expensive cars. Yes, we take glamorous trips and entertain a lot, but we haven't carried on a real conversation in years. I voted NO. I'm sure he would vote NO too."

Thousands of NO voters bluntly stated that sex was the major problem. Most women complained about the absence or infrequency of sexual relations, while the men were critical of the quality. ("She wants the lights out, the kids asleep, and the phone taken off the hook. I have to shave and shower. All this for the deadest three minutes you can imagine.")

A man who voted HELL NO in Salem, Oregon, added: "Marriage is the only war where you sleep with the enemy. And sleep is all I get."

A male from Traverse City, Michigan, wrote: "YES. She's a great girl. I would marry her again, but I'd poison her mother first."

I suppose that more good stories and jokes have been told about marriage than any other human institution, but these days folks aren't laughing quite so loudly. We want good marriages because we know that this is good, not only for family life but for society. Strong marriages are like a glue that helps hold our society together. We need stable marriages. Indeed, Dr. Glaser (of Reality Therapy fame) has said that our "number one need is to love and to be loved." Although we have witnessed a 78 percent jump in the number of single adults between 1970 and 1980, still the great majority of Americans eventually seek to find that love which they need in marriage.

For at least every two marriages nowadays, there is a divorce. But, as if to verify the old, old saying, "You can't live with them and you can't live without them," most people who divorce eventually remarry.

These are uncertain times for married folk in the United States. We fear for our marriages. We don't want to experience that eventual "breakdown of communication" one hears so much about. When the irate husband spends the night on the couch, he is not only angry, but most often also afraid, fearful that the marriage might not last.

No, we don't want our marriages to fail, but more young couples now entering marriage are expecting failure than ever before. I was involved with a young couple recently who, prior to their wedding, had actually negotiated and signed a legal agreement stipulating the conditions of a divorce settlement should their marriage not work out. This did not imply, they said, that they expected their marriage to fizzle, but the boy had been deeply hurt by his own parents' painful divorce and wanted to guard against as much damage as possible, if his marriage should not last.

Our marriages are under great pressure. The jobs we have make high demands of us; more and more husbands and wives are both employed (60 percent of the women in our own parish are employed); casual extramarital relationships are always easily available; husbands and wives are frequently separated, particularly in the military; and divorce is much more acceptable and easier to arrange nowadays. All these factors are increasing the chance of marital breakdown.

Children do not make marriage any easier, particularly in such a child-oriented era as this is. We seem to be compulsively transporting our kids to one music lesson soccer practice after another. One haggard young mother, when completing an information sheet, described her current address as "a 1978 blue Chevrolet station wagon."

At one time, people spoke of marriages as "made in heaven," yet now we are wondering, "Is there any such thing?" Does God have anything to say or does He offer any hope for all of this?

There are three major things God has shown us about marriage. The first is that *marriage is good.* Because it was "not good that man should be alone," God instituted marriage. Marriage did not just *develop,* but was ordained by God. It is not just a common-law arrangement, but a publicly celebrated, sacred *covenant* that binds a man and woman for life.

> And He [Jesus] answered and said, "Have you not read, that He who created them from the beginning made them male and female, and said, 'For this cause a man shall leave his father and mother, and shall cleave to his wife; and the two shall become one flesh'? Consequently they are no more two, but one flesh. What therefore God has joined together, let no man separate" (Matt. 19:4-6).

This was the culmination of God's initial creative activity here on the earth and, as such, it was good.

This covenant of marriage—this public binding—is for the *good* of those being married. It is like a strong wall built around the couple to keep them together even when times are difficult.

When asked how she felt about finally being married, a girl who had been living with her boyfriend for a number of years said simply: "It feels wonderful; at last I feel secure." The marriage covenant can do that for a couple.

The second thing we are told about marriage, in the Bible, is that it is a partnership between two equals. This is nowhere stated more clearly than in the opening chapters of Genesis: "And God created mankind in His own image . . . male and female He created them" (Gen. 1:27).

Both are created in the image of God with neither being better than or superior to the other.

Again, look at the second chapter of Genesis:

> Then the Lord God said, "It is not good that the man should be alone; I will make him a helper fit for him." . . . So the Lord God caused a deep sleep to fall upon the man, and while he slept took one of his ribs and closed up its place with flesh; and the rib which the Lord God had taken from the man he made into a woman and brought her to the man. Then the man said, "This at last is bone of my bones and flesh of my flesh; she shall be called Woman, because she was taken out of Man." Therefore a man leaves his father and mother and cleaves to his wife, and they become one flesh.

As we have noted, the word translated "fit" is also understood to mean "suitable" or "corresponding to" and literally implies a perfect match; a counterpart that is perfectly suited just as a key is perfectly suited to its corresponding lock. In marriage God desires that we learn to complement one another as co inheritors of His grace. This concept is further emphasized in the taking of the "rib" from which to create the wife. As the ancient rabbis pointed out, she was not taken from the head to dominate him intellectually nor was she taken from his feet to signify domination, but she was taken from his side to indicate that the wife is to stand beside the husband, arm in arm, equals under God.

In this same passage, God then brings the woman to the man, as a father escorts his daughter down the aisle at a wedding, to present her to her intended who exclaims, "This is now bone of my bone; flesh of my flesh," *again* emphasizing the perfect oneness and unity that God desires in marriage.

The "leaving" of parents and "cleaving" to one's partner indicate the sacredness of the marriage event itself and the becoming "one flesh" occurs only as the couple have been given by parents in the marriage and have finally made their covenant together. When a man and a woman are thus married, they can be "naked" and yet not ashamed.

The third major thing we learn about marriage from Scripture is that it is permanent. "What God has joined together, let no one put asunder," said Christ, and when questioned about the allowance for divorce in the Old Testament, Christ's response was to point out that "from the beginning it has not been this way." Moses had, he said, allowed divorce only because he knew full well the "hardness of men's hearts" (Matt. 19:1–9).

Christian marriage, as one person has put it, is a "permanent, unconditional, loving commitment between an imperfect man and woman."

Although we know full well that God's desire is for marriages to be permanent, loving partnerships, we also know that, as often as not, marriages don't work out and divorce occurs. Those among us who have been touched by divorce, hate it, and are not surprised to read of the prophet Malachi's telling us that God "hates divorce" as well:

> And this again you do. You cover the Lord's altar with tears, with weeping and groaning because he no longer regards the offering or accepts it with favor at your hand. You ask, "Why does he not?" Because the Lord was witness to the covenant between you and the wife of your youth, to whom you have been faithless, though she is your companion and your wife by covenant. Has not the one God made and sustained for us the spirit of life? And what does he desire? Godly offspring. So take heed to yourselves, and let none be faithless to the wife of his youth. "For I hate divorce, says the Lord the God of Israel, and covering one's garment with violence, says the Lord of Hosts. So take heed to yourselves and do not be faithless" (Mal. 2:13–16).

I have heard it said that the divorce rate has risen nearly one thousand percent in this century. Even when it occurs for the best of reasons, divorce still is something like a stingray—blistering, stinging and poisoning all who are touched by it. Divorce results too often in weighty financial burdens, insecurity among children, and severe emotional wrenching, as evidenced in heartbreak, loneliness, intense feelings of guilt, and loss of self-confidence from which some never recover. The loneliness which results from divorce can be dangerous. The divorced and widowed have much higher mortality rates than the general population. Divorced women are three times more likely to commit suicide than married women. People with weak social ties have a higher mortality rate than people with strong ties. *(Families Magazine,* May 1983). In some rare instances, divorce appears to be the best option, but it is always painful. Recently, I received the following letter from an old friend:

Dear John,

Thank you for the kind words. I appreciated your letter. I've thought about you and Susan and reached out to you so many times in my thoughts. In reality, I didn't know what to say to you and felt vaguely uneasy about saying anything at all. I've run the gamut of emotions. I've felt shame and regret, grief and euphoria. I've felt above it all and below it all, played the victim and been the victimizer. Thank God—and I do—I can admit to that. I have, once and for all, relinquished the burden of trying to be a perfect person. "And the truth shall set you free . . .' Amen! The good Lord really is smarter than I am!

Divorce is nasty business. It's death by inches. Joe and I took a long time at it. Letting the spectre hover over us, taking a slow, insidious toll. I think Joe made the decision to get out of the marriage five years ago and was just biding his time.

Marriage is time consuming. Joe wanted the trappings of wife and family without the commitment. By his own admission, he has always been on the fast track, running in hot pursuit, for whatever reason, after money and power and fame, however fleeting. He was bedazzled by the tinsel and glitter of the environment he found himself in in California. He got greedy. He'd climbed the mountain . . . all by himself. To stay there, Joe told me, was going to take all of his energy, all of his commitment. I was in the way. I made him unhappy. I kept him from being himself. I took him away from what he saw as the true purpose in his life. And he opted out.

I have resentment about that, John, despite the fact I know I set myself up for it. I didn't trust Joe not to hurt me. I was lonely in our marriage. It showed. I asked more of Joe than he was willing or able to give. He disappointed me; I disappointed him.

When Joe asked me for a divorce last spring, nevertheless, I was stunned. I forced him into counseling. To say the least, he was reluctant. It didn't work out. To survive, I had to let go. That wasn't easy. I felt bereft. I grieved for myself. I grieved for the children. I grieved for Joe. I went through lots of "what ifs" and "if onlys." I shed gallons of tears. And I waited . . . I suppose I was waiting for Joe to come to his senses. That was fantasy and a form of denial. I realized that only on the day in August I stood before the judge alone and he handed me the decree (signed officially in triplicate) of divorcement, custody and support. I felt like God had abandoned me.

That, of course, was not the case. I know that. I believe that. Most of all, I believe that God loves me and that He has forgiven me. I think I've just about forgiven myself and I'm getting closer and closer to forgiving Joe, too. The latter has been slower in coming. But come it will. I'm determined. Forgiveness, after all, *is* the best revenge.

I still have some trouble from time to time in seeing God's purpose in all this. The pain at times has been almost intolerable. I've talked to the rector at my church here about it. He likens this time in my life to being in the desert . . . he's probably right. I've had a lot of things to divest myself of. One step at a time, I'm making progress and I'm finding that I like the me that is struggling for new definition. I'm certainly not unique. God is no excepter of persons. I'm not an entity unto myself. I'm not self-sufficient. I never will be. I am finally beginning to understand what faith and trust is all about. Good has to follow . . . God has promised. I just wish He'd hurry up! Well, there it is: As you well know, I've always had a problem with patience. . . .

Pray for me, John. I'm asking the Lord for better ears with which to hear Him, for the strength to follow Him and for a kindly man to share my life with and to father my children.

The obvious implications of this are that we should take great care in the choice of a mate, but once a decision has been made, both husband and wife should commit to make of their marriage the best they possibly can and never entertain the possibility of divorce. A few years back I ran across the following quote which, although probably misleading and somewhat deceptive, nevertheless got my attention.

> Using statistics from the mid-70s, Columbia University sociologist Amitai Etzioni predicted that through family breakups America would run out of families before it runs out of oil. In 1975 the most pessimistic projection by the U.S. Census Bureau showed that by 1990 only 61 percent of all households would be husband-wife families. If, however, the present accelerating rate of erosion continues, there will be no husband-wife families by the year 2008. (*Dads Only,* June 1980)

I remember once when we were newlyweds and had had one of those traumatic arguments that always come as such a shock to young couples, Susan sobbed, "Maybe we should never have gotten married in the first place." Somewhere from within the depths of me a great instinct said, "No! Never say that. With God's help we can work it out." This I believe deeply, and have not yet seen a marriage that could not be strong where both husband and wife were committed to that goal and sought God's help.

After nearly forty years of marriage, my mother-in-law commented sadly on the number of couples breaking up, "They will never learn the joy of working and growing through these problems, and through them achieve the deeper love that *is* possible."

Some counselors feel that the unhappiest person in America, on average, is the woman who is now alone, having launched her last child.

It is likely that among those who read this, there will be some who have already failed in their marriage; perhaps it has broken apart or is even now in the process. This is *not* the end of the world. With God there *is* hope and there is forgiveness. With God's help you can rebuild your marriage. But it will take time, honesty and the help of caring Christian friends. God is not looking for the perfect marriage; he is much more concerned about the person who knows he or she has failed but is seeking his help. He can bring about true progress in such situations. According to a recent survey by *The Ladies Home Journal,* half of the happily married women in America today have, at one time or another, seriously considered divorce (June, 1980; p. 89). Progress *is* possible.

What *is* a good marriage? Is it one in which there is no conflict? No hurt? No heartache? No miscommunication? Hardly. In fact, all of these negatives *can* be helpful factors in building a good marriage, if they are viewed as opportunities for growth.

It seems to me that a good marriage is one in which, as time goes by, there is not only a deepening mutual love which is demonstrated in innumerable deeds and words, but also there is a greater sense of *satisfaction* in one's marriage relationship.

This "marital satisfaction" has been measured statistically by sociologists, and it is interesting to see what their findings are, as expressed in the following chart. (Please note, this chart represents *intact* marriages, marriages that have survived the tests. It is provided by Dennis Guernsey, a professor at Fuller Theological Seminary in California).

Each stage represented on the chart involves the gaining and releasing of a new role. It's enough to make one decide not to have children at all, especially when you learn that childless couples do not experience the dramatic dip which accompanies the bearing and raising of children. The obvious conclusion is that unless parents learn the new roles that children demand of them, children will undoubtedly decrease marital satisfaction. In any marriage, children bring stress and strain. They can also bring to a marriage a whole new dimension of joy and love that many parents would never want to be without.

For many newlyweds, all this is totally unexpected. Therefore, the *first* crucial turning point in a marriage comes when a husband and wife learn to develop realistic, shared expectations.

MEETING AND DISCUSSION

1. What kind of preparation were you given for marriage ahead of time? By whom? Your parents? Church? School? Others?

2. What were some of the biggest surprises you encountered in the first year or so?

3. What are some ingredients in the "good marriage"?

4. How does Christian marriage, as described in this chapter, differ from the typical secular view of marriage, in your opinion?

5. How do you respond to the marital satisfaction chart?

6. What is one way in which your children are making it difficult right now for your marriage? How are you seeking to deal with this? How have others dealt with this?

PHASE-LIFE CYCLE	I FIRST MARRIED	II FIRST CHILD	III YOUNG CHILDREN	IV FIRST TEENAGER	V EMPTY NEST	VI RETIREMENT
WIFE'S TASKS	ESTABLISH INTIMACY →	→ CHILDREN →	RE-EVALUATE COMMITMENT →	ESTABLISH IDENTITY →	MENOPAUSE RENEW INTIMACY →	LOSS OF SPOUSE DEVELOP INTEGRITY
HUSBAND'S TASKS	ESTABLISH IDENTITY → CAREER →		RE-EVALUATE COMMITMENT →	→ CHILDREN →	METAPAUSE ESTABLISH INTIMACY → → AGING PARENTS	LOSS OF SPOUSE REWORK IDENTITY DEVELOP INTEGRITY

MARITAL SATISFACTION: high / medium / low (curve starts high, drops through phases II–IV, rises at V, dips at VI)

CHAPTER 5

What Did You Expect?

When entering marriage, we all inevitably bring certain expectations which, if met, will result in happiness and, if not met, will lead to unhappiness. What is also inevitable is that *your* expectations will conflict with your mate's, and we need to learn quickly how to come to a common understanding.

Some of the most common conscious expectations that individuals bring to marriages (suggested by Dennis Guernsey and others) follow:

—A mate who will be loyal, devoted, loving, and exclusive; someone with whom to grow and develop.

—A constant support against the rest of the world. Spouses are expected to stand by each other in times of need, whether the adversity derives from external sources, such as loss of a job or an encounter with the law, or from within, as in the case of physical or mental illness.

—Companionship and insurance against loneliness.

—Marriage as a goal in itself rather than a beginning. Some people do not think beyond the wedding day. They assume that in some magical fashion they will live happily ever after once they are actually married.

—A panacea for the chaos and strife in one's life. All will now be calm and orderly.

—Sanctioned and readily available sex.

—Creation of a family and the experience of reproducing and participating in the growth and development of children.

—A home; a refuge from the world.

—A respectable position and status in society. Many people feel that there is a certain status in being married, in being or having a wife or husband.

—That marriage lends purpose to the lives of most people. Without it, many believe (correctly or not) that they do not have a purpose.

—A respectable cover for aggressive drives. Competitive and hostile characteristics are rationalized as being for the good of the family. Marriage supplies a socially-acceptable channel for aggressive impulses, since providing for and protecting one's family, home and possessions are sanctioned and encouraged.

How well couples come to understand each other's marital expectations, and how they learn to share the same expectations will lead them to develop one of the following five styles of marriage (G.F. Cuber and Peggy Harroff, *Sex and the Significant American,* Penguin, Baltimore, 1965).

1. THE CONFLICT-HABITUATED

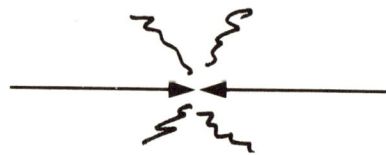

The way of life for the conflict-habituated couple is quarreling, nagging and "throwing up the past." This kind of hostility may characterize a marriage from the beginning or it may develop in the absence of proper interpersonal maintenance.

2. THE DEVITALIZED

This couple may be characterized to varying degrees with such things as little time spent together, sexual relations that are less satisfying, and interests and activities that are not shared. This style has been referred to as the "empty shell."

3. THE PASSIVE-CONGENIAL

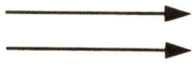

The passive-congenial is very similar to the devitalized style. The difference is that the devitalized style has known better days and is unhappy with the present state. The passive-congenial style usually choose this style because they have other commitments. Note, they are not conflicted. They do not come in contact. This is sometimes called the "parallel" style.

4. THE VITAL

The vital couple are fulfilled with one another. They share much of their life in intimate contact, but have other interests, too.

5. THE TOTAL

The total relationship is like the vital only the couple is closer. This is rare. The couple finds most *all* of their fulfillment together.

I'd like to suggest that before we move on to examine the other four turning points in marriage, you take time to ask, "What are my expectations from marriage?"

Dr. Clifford Adams of the Pennsylvania State University devised a test for married couples to help them articulate and better understand their own needs. He listed six ingredients of marriages in random order: home and family, encouraging helpmate, security, companionship, sex, love and affection. According to an article *Family Life Today* magazine, six thousand couples ranked them individually in order of importance. They then ranked them in the order they thought their spouse considered them important, and the results were surprising. While women chose love and affection as the most desired ingredient in marriage, men chose companionship. Husbands and wives totally misread their mate's preferences. Wives thought their husbands would put sex at the top of the list while men chose home and family as greatest in importance for their wives. The actual preferences were as follows:

Men	Women
1. Companionship	1. Love and affection
2. Sex	2. Security
3. Love and affection	3. Companionship
4. Home and family	4. Home and family
5. Encouraging helpmate	5. Encouraging helpmate
6. Security	6. Sex

Many couples never seem ever to get around to discussing these expectations, and this, as one would expect, leads inevitably to an unsatisfying marriage. Dr. Selma Miller, president of the Association of Marriage and Family Counselors, states: "The most common cause of marriage problems is that partners' needs are in conflict, but they can't discuss the conflict because they don't know one exists. They only know they are miserable."

As I have thought about it, the expectations I had for my wife, upon first entering marriage, were ludicrous. I expected her to hold down an emotionally draining, full-time job, keep an immaculate home, work in the church with me, prepare meals like Mom (Mom had a full-time cook, I later remembered!), always be as sexy as Bo Derek, but also be as pious as the Virgin Mary! All of this, of course, assumed too that she would never get tired and she would always accept me totally as I was.

Martin Luther loved to describe marriage as the "school for character," and now in these years since we were married, with the coming of five children, I have been *educated* in this school. My initial expectations have changed. Marriage is not much like I expected—it's a lot harder, but infinitely better, too.

Before your meeting, let me suggest that you take time to complete the test devised by Dr. Adams to evaluate *your* needs and those of your spouse.

MEETING AND DISCUSSION

1. What ideas in the reading we've been doing this week struck you as particularly important?

2. If you completed the little test from Penn State University, what discoveries did you make, if any, about your expectations in marriage?

3. What do you feel are some of the most persistent obstacles to having a truly satisfying marriage? What about in your *own* marriage? (If divorced or widowed, perhaps share from your years of marriage.)

4. What would you say is the most important principle you have learned so far about how to have a good marriage, and how do you aim to begin working toward this personally?

Close by taking time to express any other particular concerns for which persons would like prayer. Then remember one another's specific needs in a quiet, informal time of conversational prayer around the circle.

CHAPTER 6

Valuing Our Differences*

Once a husband and wife begin to clearly enunciate their expectations for marriage, it becomes more and more clear that we are so different from one another. The second turning point is precisely in this regard.

The sociologist Virginia Satir has said that "two people are first interested in each other because of their sameness, but they remain interested over the years because of their differences." One of the first areas in which we are different from one another is in our perceptions of our own role as opposed to the role of our mate. These assumptions that we bring into marriage are usually based upon observation of our own parents. After all, they are the ones who, more than anyone else, demonstrate to us what a father and husband, or what a wife and mother is to be like. They are our role models.

Often I say to young couples, "If you want to get some idea of what your marriage will be like, you (pointing to the man) imagine *your* father married to *her* mother!" This never falls to produce *some* sort of interesting response. Even in the case of the person who has consciously rejected the style or personality of his own parent, there still remains a strong influence. You are your parents' child.

This was vividly brought to my attention one night when I arrived home at dinnertime and noticed that my wife seemed unusually cool toward me. I did a quick mental rechecking of the day, noting that we

---

*If you are studying this in a group, read Chapters 6, 7 and 8 prior to the next meeting.

had been good friends when I left in the morning, I had called her from work to say "hello," and to the best of my knowledge, there was nothing wrong. But, boy, was something wrong! Valuing her right to privacy, I said nothing but redoubled my efforts all through a rather icy dinner to be the cheerful, loving, model husband.

After bathing the children, putting them to bed, and returning to help in the kitchen, I ventured to ask, "Sweetheart, I've noticed that you are a little quiet tonight and am just wondering if anything is wrong."

She looked at me as though I had rocks instead of brains, and finally, in great indignation, said:

"It's the dishwasher!" (as though that perfectly explained the entire matter).

"The dishwasher?" I said.

"Yes," she said. "You knew all day long that the dishwasher was broken, I told you this morning and you haven't done a *thing* about it."

I really am a slow learner and the full significance of this revelation still did not sink in, so I said, quite sincerely, "Well, yes, I do remember now. Didn't you call the repairman? Didn't he show up?"

Now *she* was the one who was shocked, for she said, "Well, no, I didn't call the repairman. That's *your* job—you are the husband. You are the one who is supposed to take care of things like that."

By this time, even *my* feeble brain had begun to perceive what was happening and I had a mental picture of my father-in-law covered with grease, a wrench and screwdriver in hand, working away on a broken dishwasher. Then, I thought of my own father in a similar circumstance. *At last* I saw the root of the whole problem. I never recalled my father fixing anything around the house (although he certainly must have). If the oven was broken or some appliance needed fixing, my mother would always call the shop and someone would come attend to the problem. But not Susan's dad. He is a true Mr. Fixit.

It had not even occurred to me that my wife expected me to do anything about the dishwasher, whereas she assumed I would handle everything. Once I saw what was happening, I had a good laugh about it, although my wife didn't think it nearly so funny.

How many conflicts can be avoided if we can just begin to communicate our *differing role expectations* of one another! Now this is but one way in which husbands and wives differ; there must be countless other ways too.

One other example that has been an important area of difference between us has to do with our abilities. I married a very capable woman. She is an unusually gifted person, particularly in the areas of administration and organization, public speaking and interpersonal relations. Before we were married, she had already established her own reputation as a Christian leader and speaker. I greatly admired these gifts and her remarkably quick and bright mind—that is, until we had been married a few months when gradually I began to be threatened by all her abilities. I was in seminary then, and was struggling along as a student assistant in a large East Coast Church. Planning ahead, writing sermons and organizing events did not come easily to me.

Before very long, it became clear that my wife was much further along in these areas than I was. She could think through a Bible passage and write out a crakerjack sermon outline (complete with three points and three illustrations) in about fifteen minutes. She could visualize the needs of the youth group and put together in her mind an excellent plan for a weekend retreat, while I was still trying to decide which weekend we should go! As I realized what was happening, I began to be more and more threatened. *I* was the theological student, *I* was the one who had to preach, *I* was supposed to be the great spiritual leader (and besides all that *I* was a man!). Really, it was looking bad for old number one, for he was being bested in all his areas of *supposed* expertise. All of a sudden, my wife seemed to be more my *rival* than my partner.

I don't know how many couples struggle with this, but in the era of increasing participation of women in the marketplace, I would guess that there are a lot of husbands or wives running around quite threatened by their mates. But how ridiculous! God gives us *partners,* not rivals. And when our partners have gifts that *we* do not have ourselves, how much better off are we! Slowly, imperceptibly, it began to dawn on me that the Lord had given me a mate who could do some things better than I could, not to embarrass me, but to *help* me. And eventually, I even began to see that there were a few areas in which I seemed to have strengths where she was not so strong. It was a great day for us both, for instance, when I acknowledged that she was a better bookkeeper than I, and she began to balance the checkbook.

In the marvelous economy of God, a husband and wife can actually enhance one another's personal security rather than threaten one another. We are *made* to "complete" one another. We are more effective together than we could be apart as single people.

Perhaps more often than we realize, our different expectations of each other, or our different perceptions of our own roles, cause us to become angry with each other. If we can just pull back and ask ourselves, *"Why* does this bother me so much?" we will almost invariably realize that the anger is unjustified and based on some valid *difference* between the husband and wife.

The other day I was somewhat irritated at the complete and utter mess in my wife's car. There were paper cups, school papers, Rice Crispies, broken pencils, old half-eaten suckers, and an incredible array of other assorted items of trash from one end to the other. "Why in the *world* is her car always so messy!" My mind reflected, "I don't remember *my mother's* car being a mess when I was a kid. This is terrible!" Then I stopped and examined my attitude and asked, "Why?"

The reason the car is a mess is that she is always carting around five children. *"Your* car would look like this too," I thought to myself, "if you did all that carpooling." In fact the more I thought about it, the more I realized that *probably* even my *mother's* car would've been a mess if she had had so many little children to carry around! So, on the spot, I shrugged it off and got the trash can and cleaned out her car for her. It made *me* feel better and demonstrated to her in a small way that I care about her.

Having said all this, it should be noted that anger is not necessarily a bad thing in marriage. God gets angry; Christ got angry. Anger is often appropriate in marriage if it's directed at something that is wrong; if it is controlled; and if it contains no hatred or resentment. Too often we become angry because of misunderstandings and mistaken assumptions. But even then, such occasions *can* help us ultimately to get to know one another better.

Most of the time, I observe that couples who have strong marriages become angry generally out of tiredness. I have never lived in any other generation than my own, and cannot substantiate my opinion that we are the busiest generation yet. But our busyness, our hurriedness, our incredible pursuit of the fulfillment of all the possibilities around us is exhausting. And when we are exhausted, we must learn to tell our mates that this is the case (they will probably already have perceived it)—to say, "Honey, I don't mean to be snappish or angry. I really *do* love you, but I am so tired and irritable tonight. Please just know that I don't mean anything by it and forgive me."

CHAPTER 7

Deepening the Love Relationship

Christian couples should be the most loving people in the world. Almost invariably, after a couple has been married for awhile and the initial freshness has begun to wear off, the romantic hue begins to fade. Generally it is the husband, rather than the wife, who settles into a familiar, predictable pattern, while often the wife longs for him to court her and surprise her as he did when they were just sweethearts. For many married folk, it has been my observation that a need remains for a romantic touch in the relationship. This is not always true, certainly, but it is interesting to see that even in the Bible place is given for this sort of expression in marriage.

Read the following quote from the Song of Solomon, as the King praises his wife for her beauty:

> How beautiful you are, my love! How your eyes shine with love behind your veil. Your hair dances like a flock of goats bounding down the hills of Gilead. Your teeth are as white as sheep that have just been shorn and washed . . . they are all perfectly matched. Your lips are like a scarlet ribbon; how lovely they are when you speak. Your checks glow behind your veil. Your neck is like the tower of David, round and smooth, with a necklace like a thousand shields hung around it. Your breasts are like gazelles, twin deer feeding among the lilies. I will stay on the hill of myrrh, the hill of incense, until the morning breezes blow and the darkness disappears. How beautiful you are, my love; how perfect you are! . . . Your love delights me, my sweetheart and bride. Your love is better than

wine; your perfume more fragrant than any spice. The taste of honey is on your lips, my darling; your tongue is milk and honey for me. Your clothing has all the fragrance of Lebanon. My sweetheart, my bride, is a walled garden, a private spring . . . (Song of Solomon 4:1–7, 10–12).

It is hard to imagine such romantic expressions and sexual allusions in the Word of God, but deep appreciation and responsiveness to one's spouse is, I believe, usually quite vital.

While the traditional roles of the housewife in the home and the husband on the job are rapidly changing, a pattern which marriage counselors are quite familiar with in troubled marriages is that of a man whose main concern is his *work* while the wife's major concern is for her husband and children. Many men can be content with a business partnership sort of relationship with their wives, for they see their wives as companions and as bed partners. As long as the children and home are cared for, the meals are provided, and he is being satisfied in bed, many a husband is quite happy; romance is nice, but not necessary. This sort of on-the-surface relationship drives many wives crazy. They crave something more meaningful and want very much to be the special sweethearts of their husbands. They want to be respected, appreciated and loved with tenderness. Certainly a wife who does not get this from her husband will find it almost impossible to communicate further the desire for romance. And when she tries, the husband too often misunderstands and thinks that an occasional box of candy or bouquet of flowers is all she needs. What she wants is a little time with her husband, to be *cared* for, to be told tenderly how precious she is, how wonderful she is. She wants to be courted.

In the television series, *Winds of War,* there was the following classic line. Rhoda, who is married to Pug, the typical close-mouthed, gruff, Navy captain, eventually falls in love with Palmer, the widower who came to Berlin on business; in explaining to Palmer just how she had fallen in love with him, she says, "Palmer, in college, Pug courted me and he won me. But now, Pug shuts me out. When we were in Berlin, *you* courted me and you won me."

Apparently, Palmer did it, not on purpose, but simply by treating her as a lady, by spending time with her, and by listening and sharing with her—all of which her husband had quit doing years before.

Certainly the reasons Herman Wouk included this conversation in his novel is that, over and over, he had observed this very same thing happening to his married friends and acquaintances. A man needs to learn to encourage his wife and build her up, particularly if she is harried by small children, and even before the children come. In the Old Testament, there is a law that God established for His people in their early days that says, "A newly married man is not to be drafted into the army, nor given any other responsibilities for a year. He shall be free to be at home, happy to be with his wife" (Deuteronomy 24:5). The King James Version says, "He shall cheer the wife whom he hath taken." Certainly this was one way of encouraging the successful growth of the Jewish people and ensuring that they would "be fruitful and multiply," but it says more than that.

The husband has a certain responsibility for the emotional well-being of his wife, and romance is a vital element in this well-being. This is not to say that the responsibility is not reciprocal, also—the wife is to live with her husband's needs and desires uppermost in her mind (Eph. 5), but in our Western culture I often sense that the greater need for this active sort of love and encouragement is felt by the wife and mother.

In the last decade, millions of wives have begun to enter the marketplace with the result being not only more working mothers and wives, but also a dramatic increase in the likelihood of husbands and wives losing touch with one another. The more time the wife and mother spends working outside the home, the greater the need for romance in the marriage.

How do we men develop this sense of appreciation in our marriages? Consider something as simple as a hug. The following quotes were in an article in a local paper:

> Dr. Marc H. Hollender, chairman of the department of psychiatry at Vanderbilt University School of Medicine in Nashville, for the past dozen years has studied the role of hugging between adult men and women.
>
> In snuggling up to her husband, Hollender says, the wife may be seeking "a sense of closeness" or a feeling of "being protected, feeling secure, being loved." What she may not want at this particular moment is sex.
>
> Women, he says, appear "able to separate the wish to be held as an end in itself from the wish to be held as a prelude to sex." While many men may initially make the same differentiation, they "may be less able to hold to it than women." For men, "Being held and holding is much more likely to lead to sexual arousal."
>
> "When a woman wishes to be cuddled and nothing more," says Hollender, "her message may be, and often is, misunderstood by her husband. She separates her desire to be held from her wish for sexual activity; her husband is much less likely to do so."
>
> In a series of studies over the years involving more than 1000 women (and men), Hollender has tried to "find out how important

their wish was to be held or cuddled and what they would do to get it fulfilled."

To some, the idea of research into hugging may sound fanciful, but for Hollender, "The more we understand about people's needs, desires and wishes and how they affect relationships, the more they can be helped." (The Washington Post; February 2, 1981)

We must "cherish" our wives and let them know that we love them by recalling the sorts of surprises and love offerings that pleased them most during our dating days. We must be in touch with them, even if just by telephone, and tell them we love them. If we can do some specific deed each day that says, "I love you," it will help give them the encouragement they need and show them that they are truly the queens in our lives.

I have known some couples for which the very opposite was true. The wife was the business-oriented one while the husband longed for more of an emotional involvement. Whichever is the case in your marriage, a consistently creative approach to romancing our mates will pay rich dividends, going a long way toward building a secure emotional wall around our marriages. The whole idea leads very naturally to the next turning point.

CHAPTER 8

Learning to Be Together

A study of married couples by speech communications expert Ray Birdwhistell, as reported in *Impact* magazine, reveals that couples spend an average of only 27.5 minutes per week talking to each other. One reason, he reported, was that the average household television is on forty-six hours a week. *(Dads Only,* August 1980).

Unless we develop the sort of schedule that enables us to have regular consistent, in-depth time of communication with each other, the romancing we have talked about will be shallow and nearly meaningless. Breakdown in communication and loss of shared interests and goals are the two most common reasons for broken marriages. In fact, all five ingredients which psychologists tell us lie at the base of marital disintegration center around the loss of interpersonal communication. (The other three are sexual incompatibility, infidelity, and excitement lost in marriage.)

There are two basic sorts of relationships between friends, according to sociologists—primary relationships and secondary relationships. A primary relationship is a close, intimate sharing in which the two persons share their lives in a significant way (this doesn't necessarily have to do with sex). They have moved away from the superficial relationship where conversation consists mainly of cliches and an abbreviated reporting of facts, to a meaningful sharing of not only information, but thoughts, feelings and concerns. Primary relationships are vital, alive and deep. Secondary relationships are shallow and functional; only superficial interaction occurs.

Apparently, in many instances, Americans are becoming more and more a people of secondary rather than primary relationships. We are losing our ability to have intimacy because of all the things pulling us apart. In our family life, we only see each other passing in the night or at quick meals between more and more commitments. Loneliness in our society is reaching epidemic proportions. The average American moves thirteen times in his lifetime. Studies at the University of Michigan recently indicate that Americans today are less integrated into the social structure. They don't participate and they don't feel needed. Our cities are impersonal, and electronic entertainment often replaces one-to-one conversations. (*Families Magazine,* May 1983).

Children only complicate this problem. On a recent all-too-typical Saturday (not to mention the regular weekday scramble), I had a speaking engagement at 9:00, a responsibility to help lead a Little League parade at 9:45 (on the other side of town), a wedding at noon (followed by a reception naturally), and a T-Ball game (I'm a coach) at 4:30. In the meantime, the twins had a party at 10:00, my sons were in the parade at 9:45, another child had a Sunday school outing at 11:30, and my oldest daughter had tap dancing at 12:00. Susan had an important commitment at 2:00, and during all of this I'm worrying about the sermon for Sunday which just hadn't fallen into place. In the midst of all this confusion, the hot water heater burst and flooded the basement, and our golden retriever escaped from her pen! We try to avoid days like that, but unfortunately for parents, they are more and more typical, and it is nearly impossible to experience primary relationships amid such a schedule.

Our family lives in an area that is absolutely overwhelming in terms of the ever-present opportunities for educational and broadening experiences. Our children are surely the most entertained and broadly experienced in our nation's history. We want to give them all the opportunities we possibly can, but soon we become tyrannized by the family's various schedules and we lose touch with one another. Add to this the new element of mother working outside the home and the increasing tension brought on by day-care center living and babysitting and you have a boiling cauldron of family activity. Even for families where the mothers are not employed, the rising demand for volunteers (accelerated by the shortage of non-employed mothers) is taking mothers away from home as never before.

It is absolutely essential that we do *not* let our commitments rob us of significant family life, and we can only do this by understanding that time together as husbands and wives, parents and children, is just as valuable as all of the other activities. If there is little sharing of thoughts, hopes, hurts, decisions or anxieties, there is little relationship and we become the "anonymous generation"—a well-educated, broadly involved, busy bunch of unknowns!

Earlier, I mentioned an article in *Redbook* magazine (August 1981), entitled "What Makes a Good Family?" In it was reported that two professors (Stinnett and DeFrain, Department of Human Development and the Family, College of Home Economics, University of Nebraska) completed a study designed to look at some successfully happy families to establish what behavior or characteristics they had in common. The study was called the "National Study of Family Strengths." Stinnett and De Frain located 350 families all over the country who were willing to participate in the study and who met four basic criteria:

1. All couples considered themselves happily married.

2. They were satisfied with the parent-child relationships in the family.

3. For the sake of study uniformity, all the marriages had to be first marriages.

4. The families had to be intact.

Sixty percent of the participants were from urban areas. All socio-economic groups were represented and were mostly in the middle-income range. The age range stretched from mid-20s to 60s and included Blacks, Poles, Jews, Italians and Hispanics.

The basic findings included:

1. Happy families spend more time together.

2. Happy families have good communication patterns. They spend a lot of time talking to each other and share their feelings, getting conflicts out into the open.

3. Happy families show appreciation for one another. (According to Stinnett, a technique used in counseling unhappy families is teaching them to notice and to praise the positive qualities in other family members.)

4. Happy families are committed to the family group. They crossed other things off the list to make more time for the family, and they tried to relieve themselves of unnecessary stress from outside.

5. Happy families tend to be religious. Most went to church or synagogue regularly, participated in other church activities, and had regular family prayer or Bible-reading sessions.

6. Happy families deal with crises positively. They had the ability to see something positive in every situation and to focus on that aspect. They joined together to face the crisis head-on.

If we do not cut back on our activities and begin to establish consistent patterns of family times together and times alone as couples, there will be more and more articles like the following excerpts from *Newsweek* magazine's "My Turn" column (Karen Kenyon) (April 30, 1979):

> On the second of November my husband did not come home from work. He was not one for dramatics, not an unpredictable or violent man. He seemed to be a good-humored, sensitive, intelligent, and utterly reliable person, until that night.
>
> Dick, the man I have lived with, loved and been married to for 16 years, the father of our 12-year-old son, had chosen to end his life. He told no one of his decision but left behind two suicide notes which we discovered by 10:00 that night. Though the campus police at the university where he worked looked for him, they found him too late. Dick had jumped from an 11-story building. It was not the act of a madman, but the act of someone scrunched in, crumpled, thwarted by his job, and by life. It was the act of a man who just didn't fight back, who just didn't, couldn't talk about what troubled him.
>
> I've found it difficult to be sensible, to avoid guilt and constant questioning. The notes Dick left said it was his job, that I had nothing to do with what he did. Still, why couldn't I have seen what was happening? Why couldn't I have saved him? He had been the best friend I ever had. I must not have been a good enough friend to him.

Again quoting Virginia Satir, "Communication is the greatest single factor affecting a person's health and his relationship to others." The implications of this statement are staggering, not only for families and marriages, but for the health of our community as well. What is perhaps not so obvious is the connection to our relationship with God. I am convinced that a major reason for the abundance of superficial Christian commitment in the West today is related to the decrease of primary relationships in general. If we don't have close relationships with people, then how can we have close relationships with God? We struggle with prayer, with listening to God, with getting quiet before God because we don't do this with *people* either.

How can we then establish stronger patterns of communication in our marriages? We have found the following three ideas to be invaluable.

1. Set aside one night a week as a "date night." Spending a lot of money on a fancy meal is not so important as getting a babysitter and getting out of the house for an evening alone. The idea is to spend a quiet, uneventful time just visiting with each other, not only getting caught up on each other's activities, but to take time to explore together some ideas, concerns or dreams that you just don't have time to dwell on normally.

We have a favorite tavern out in the Virginia countryside called the Red Fox Inn to which we love to retreat for such an evening. Our budget, however, rarely allows such extravagance and so on some Thursday nights we have a "date at the Blond Fox Inn." In other words, we stay home, charge the kids with putting themselves to bed without interrupting us, build a fire, and have a cozy dinner in the living room (in case you don't get the connection, Susan is blond!) Some of our best dates have been at home, not to mention the joy I derive in not having to take the babysitter home.

2. Plan regular escapes two or three times a year, away from home and children, for a night or two if possible. Getting good sleep and having a couple of days to enjoy each other in uninterrupted peace becomes like a little honeymoon. Most middle-class Americans, if they can't afford staying at a motel or vacation spot, have friends who have vacation homes who will gladly let them use them. Spending money on these honeymoons is not frivolous or unChristian. It is an investment in your marriage and will strengthen the fabric of your family life.

3. Perhaps most important is a habit which we have only developed in the last few years that we call our "Tea Talks." During the week, we are committed to a twenty-minute visit alone, upon my arrival at the house after work. Since my schedule demands that I be out at night so frequently, we work quite hard to maintain this time. It gives us about ten minutes apiece to tell about our day, our activities, our thoughts and feelings. But, in addition, we have taken the advice of Dr. David Mace, a Baptist marriage and family life counselor, and also try to share in two other ways—"How am I feeling about myself?" and "How am I feeling about us?"

For me, these two questions have been quite revealing, for I have never been one to pay much attention to my feelings. Whatever happens, happens. I keep on keeping on. I don't get my feelings hurt, I don't get very excited or upset—"just keep on trucking." At least so I thought, until one day, in sincerely trying to answer my wife's question as to how I felt about something, I began to realize that I *was* having some emotional ups and downs and just had not been acknowledging them. There is something very liberating and revelatory about such a discovery, not just to oneself but also to one's mate. Our communication has begun to spiral upward significantly since the advent of the "Tea Talks."

People do not simply gel into the same position, keeping the same opinions and never having feelings. All of us are constantly changing, and unless we learn to share our hearts and bear our souls with our mates, we will shut one another off and not grow together. Either you grow closer together in a marriage or you grow further apart. There is little neutral ground.

Men, you've got to realize this great need for communication and initiate it in your marriage. Don't be satisfied to be one of America's "passive men." In America, men have forgotten the need for intimate communication. This is emphasized in a recent book by Pierre Mornell, *Passive Men, Wild Women:*

> The most important part of the man's day—earning a living—is over when he hits the front door at night. However, a crucial part of the woman's day—making a connection in the relationship—is still to come. Whereas a man may get his sense of worth from work, his wife needs a sense of her worth not only from her work, but also from her relationship.... Beyond her own needs for privacy, the woman needs emotional contact with her man.
>
> The tragedy is that the man needs it too—we just never learned this. (Ballantine, 1983; p. 5)

MEETING AND DISCUSSION

As you meet tonight, reflect on your response to these chapters (6, 7 & 8).

1. What are some areas of differences in values or expectations that you discovered in your own marriage? How have you sought to come to a working agreement?

2. What are some of the most outstanding factors that curtail the romantic side of marriage? How do you seek to overcome them?

3. What traditions have you established or have you observed in other marriages that have deepened the quality of your time together?

You may decide tonight to take a little detour now, or later, and spend a session or two dealing with the common problems that plague most marriages, such as finances, time-management, etc. See the appendix for some suggestions.

4. Share any concerns dealing with family members, friends, acquaintances or upcoming events and spend some time in conversational prayer for these things.

CHAPTER 9

We Need a Shared Faith in God

Each of us is incomplete, even though we have families. No mate or child can completely satisfy us. St. Augustine wrote, "O God, our hearts are restless until they find their resting place in Thee." Pascal, the French physicist and philosopher, said, "Within the heart of every man is a God-shaped vacuum that only Jesus Christ can fill." A complete marriage is not simply horizontal but is more like a triangle; the husband and wife are not only joined together, but each one individually knows and is growing in the vertical dimension with God as well. Few of us are strong enough to maintain solid marriages today apart from the help of the Lord. He is the creator and designer of man, of woman, and of marriage itself. He knows how to make marriage work. If we are consistently seeking God's guidance and His help, it follows naturally that we will have better marriages. Only the fool says in his heart, "I do not need God."

It is of paramount importance that Christian couples learn to pray together, not just in church, not just at mealtimes, although these are assumed and rightly stressed. But further, husbands and wives can experience a whole new realm of relationship if they can learn to join together in personal prayer at other times as well.

Because I had always been in the habit of praying at bedtime, I assumed that I would continue that habit after I was married. From the first night of our honeymoon, we have consistently ended the day with an informal time of prayer after crawling into bed. It is not a time for lengthy, involved intercession, but simply a brief, personal moment of thanksgiving and supplication for ourselves and our loved ones. An unexpected byproduct

WE NEED A SHARED FAITH IN GOD

of this habit during the early years of our marriage was that it ensured we did not go to sleep angry at each other. You cannot pray with someone with whom you are angry. If you are going to pray together, you are going to have to get reconciled first. Bedtime prayer has helped us to experience the value of the biblical injunction never to go to bed angry. Not that this will always enable you blissfully to forgive and forget one another's faults or hurtful words, but it ensures that you end the day without grudges, having taken all steps possible to see that your relationship is right both with one another and with God.

Learning to pray together is, in my opinion, the most important of all these turning points. As I noted earlier, in our day, one out of every two marriages ends in divorce. According to a survey conducted by Dr. Peterim Sorokin at Harvard, only one in 1015 marriages end in divorce where couples have taken time daily to have a time of personal prayer (in Bill Bright, *The Uniqueness of Jesus;* 1968, p. 11).

Couples can begin by saying a blessing at meals or by holding hands and saying the Lord's Prayer, or by joining in the prayers of the Prayer Book. But, may I urge you further to learn to pray without written prayers—simply to express your thoughts and desires to the Lord in your own words.

The other day I was holding two small twigs and could easily break either of them in my hands. But when I pressed them along side one another and tried to break them, it was very difficult. Putting three together I found I could not break them in my fingers. That is a picture of how even in a strong marriage, when the Lord enters the relationship and comes alongside the couple and they talk with Him together, the marriage is immeasurably strengthened. It reminded me of the verse in Ecclesiastes 4:9–12:

> Two are better than one. Together they can work more effectively. If one of them falls down the other can help him up. But if someone is alone and falls, it's just too bad for there is no one to help him. If it's cold, two can sleep together and stay warm but how can you stay warm by yourself? Two can resist an attack that would defeat one alone.

Then the writer says something very interesting, for he has been extolling the value of two persons supporting one another, which, of course, is directly applicable to marriage. He concludes by writing: "A threefold cord can never be broken" (Ecclesiastes 4:12b).

That is the picture of a marriage in Christ.

Please use the following suggestions as an initial guide to begin learning more about how to pray together.

COUPLES DAILY PRAYER GUIDE

Let's set aside a time each day and use the following suggestions to help us in our efforts to pray together as couples or with our children as well.

Each Day: One of you should lead in prayer, giving thanks for specific blessings, as well as perhaps one quality you appreciate in the other. The other follows in the same way.

One confesses and asks God's forgiveness for _____ .

The other does the same.

Each prays for any particular concerns or people on their mind.

For instance, the husband might, in addition to praying for his own concerns, pray for something specific in his wife's schedule that day, while the wife might pray for a particular job situation (meeting, decision, personnel concern, etc.) facing the husband at work.

Day One: In addition to the above, your family might pray.

The Eldest Child:
1. Something I'm thankful for.
2. Behavior and attitudes.
3. Friends.
4. Physical needs.
5. School activities.
6. Spiritual growth.

Couple in our Group and their family:
1. Specific requests.
2. Their children.
3. Their growth as a family in Christ.
4. Special needs of which you are aware such as: your parents and siblings and any needs they may have; our church and any needs you're aware of there; your neighborhood friends and any needs there; persons in need of God whom you might bring to church; any national or international concerns; your future as a family (job, vacation, moves, schools, finances, children's mates, etc); any tensions in your home.

You might take turns praising God for different things in the following areas: an aspect of God's character that is meaningful to you; a quality in each other; a quality in each child; for an answered prayer; a material blessing; a person who has been a blessing or a help this week; other things.

Before the next meeting, spend some time doing the following study: Look in some detail at St. Paul's advice to husbands and wives in Ephesians 5:21–33 (read the passage in several translations). Make notes in reference to the following questions and come prepared to share your thoughts.

1. What does it mean to "submit yourselves to one another" (v.21)? What are some practical ways that wives must submit to husbands? What are some practical ways that husbands must submit to wives?

2. In verses 22–24, Paul focuses on the wife. What are reasons that make it difficult for some wives to be obedient to these commands?

3. How does Christ love the church (v. 25)? Think of as many descriptive words as you can. Which come more naturally to husbands in their relationships with their wives? Which are more difficult?

4. In verse 33, Paul stresses "love" and "respect." How are those two qualities related in the husband and wife relationship? Can they be separated?

MEETING AND DISCUSSION

You should be rotating leadership by now.

1. Take twenty minutes or so to let people tell how they have been doing in applying anything they learned in the last few chapters, or how things are going in some of the areas in which they requested prayer at a prior meeting.

2. Review the Bible study questions together.

3. Divide into two groups with all the women in one group and all the men in the other. In each group list the qualities that would describe the "perfect husband" and the "perfect wife." Then come back together and share your results. This may spark some discussion as to particular areas in which husbands and wives feel inadequate. Encourage such discussion.

4. The major point toward the end of this chapter is on the importance of praying together as couples. Ask each couple to tell if they have begun to do this and if so, how it is going; if not, try to put your finger on the factors that make this difficult for so many.

Close in prayer.

CHAPTER 10

How Does a Child Grow

The bookshelves of a good bookstore have volume upon volume of textbooks that propound theories and insights into how little ones grow up. The psychologists and the sociologists, the professional and the layman, all have their ideas—and the more one reads the more convinced one becomes that growing up is an extremely complicated affair. Yet we all do grow up somehow (or do we)? I have a forty-year-old friend who in many ways is still a rebellious teenager. You know people like this, too. Physical growth and aging does not always imply true maturation.

ERIKSON'S STAGES OF DEVELOPMENT

Erik H. Erikson, psychoanalyst and professor emeritus of developmental psychology at Harvard, has affected our thinking in this area perhaps as much as anyone since Sigmund Freud, and it is worthwhile to make a thumbnail sketch of his theories. In his book, *Childhood and Society* (Norton; 1963: pp. 247ff), he summed up his observations after fifteen years of research. He suggested that alongside the stages of psycho-sexual development described by Freud (the oral, anal, phallic, genital, oedipal and pubertal) were the psychosocial stages of ego development in which a person must develop new basic orientations to himself and to the social world around him. Added to this, he found that personality development continues throughout a person's entire life. Each stage of personality development has a positive as well as a negative aspect. He identified eight stages in the human life cycle in each of which a whole new area of "social interaction" becomes possible, both in a person's interaction with himself as well as with the society around himself. These stages are worthwhile for us to consider.

TRUST VS. MISTRUST

Throughout the first year of life, a child develops a foundational attitude toward others of trust or mistrust based on how people have related to the child during that year. If the needs and cares of the infant are generally met with care, concern and consistency, the child develops a perception of people as being basically trustworthy, helpful and dependable. On the other hand, an attitude of fear, suspicion and mistrust will develop if the child encounters rejection or inadequate or inconsistent care.

As the child matures, later experience with others may temper and supplant the attitude developed during the first year. For instance, a troubled, mistrusting child may encounter a wonderful teacher who takes great pains to care for the child and demonstrate her or his trustworthiness. On the other hand, a child who develops a strong sense of trust during infancy may have that shattered if, at a later stage, something like a bitter divorce develops between his parents.

AUTONOMY VS. DOUBT

During the second and third years, Erikson sees the development of a sense of autonomy. It is during this time that a child learns skills such as walking, climbing, talking, pushing and pulling. The typical child takes great pride in learning to do these things. Anyone who has raised a three-year-old knows well the typical "I can do it myself" attitude. Children need to develop this sense of personal autonomy or else they become doubtful of their capabilities. If those who are caring for the child impatiently refuse to let the child develop his abilities by overprotecting or continually being impatient when the child spills, breaks, wets or whatever, then the child may develop a sense of shame in respect to other people. A child who develops his self-confidence at this age will carry a sense of autonomy into later stages.

INITIATIVE VS. GUILT

Between ages four and five, most children have become capable of initiating a great variety of motor activities (running, riding a tricycle or bicycle, etc.). He does not have to imitate others but can do as he pleases. He also can initiate his own thoughts and fantasies, and express verbally with more facility. Erikson argues that it is how parents respond to these self-initiated activities that will determine whether the child develops a sense of initiative or a sense of guilt. Parents who feel that play is silly or stupid, or who consider child's questions to be annoying, may cause the child to sense a feeling of guilt at such self-initiated expressions. On the other hand, parents who answer their children's questions and encourage their social and physical initiatives will help the child become confident in initiating his or her own actions.

INDUSTRY VS. INFERIORITY

The fourth stage, stretching from six to eleven, encompasses the elementary school years when most children are spending a good deal of time outside the home. During this period of life, children learn to reason deductively and to play and learn by rules. They learn to take turns in games and play games like checkers which require obedience to regulations. Erikson says that during these years children develop a sense of industry or, on the other extreme, inferiority.

If they are encouraged to do or build practical things and to finish their projects and are praised and rewarded, the sense of industry is enhanced. (Building model planes, coloring pictures or sewing are typical projects.) If those caring for the children treat such industrial pursuit as a nuisance or simply "making a mess," the child may develop a sense of inferiority. By this time in life, the home is no longer the only major environment for the child, and the attitude of the teacher may influence the child just as much as that of the parent.

IDENTITY VS. CONFUSION

Roughly between ages twelve and eighteen (Stage 5) children move into adolescence and mature mentally as well as physiologically. In addition to the new feelings and sensations they experience as a result of changes in their bodies, they also develop new ways of looking at the world. They can think more analytically about the way other people think and live and also wonder just how others feel about them. Adolescents are able to visualize "ideals" now—ideal mates, families, societies, religions. The adolescent begins to be able to build theories and philosophies aimed at bringing the conflicting, differing aspects of society into a peaceful whole. The adolescent often becomes an impatient idealist with all the answers.

According to Erikson, young people develop either a strong sense of ego identity or a personal sense of confusion as to their own roles. The adolescent either begins to integrate all he has learned about himself in his various roles as son, brother, athlete, student, choir member, garden worker, friend, and other roles into a whole which seems to make sense, or he doesn't. He begins to have a sense of direction and purpose, or becomes more confused about who he is and where he is going.

Parents play less and less of a major role during these years while peers and models play a larger role. When there is a sense of confusion about his role a teen can develop a variety of identities or identities quite different from those prescribed by family.

If an adolescent fails to establish a clear sense of personal identity, this is not to say that later on he may not come to a clearer sense of identity. Over and over Erikson emphasizes that life constantly is changing and that inability to resolve a problem or develop sufficiently in one stage does not preclude the possibility of growing on through this successfully later on.

INTIMACY VS. ISOLATION

This stage is the one of young adulthood, a time of courtship and early family life which lasts on into early middle age. It is during this stage that persons need to develop in the interpersonal dimension of *intimacy* or else become isolated from others.

Intimacy means the ability to share and care about another person without fear of losing oneself in the process. Intimacy need not necessarily mean sexual involvement; it can be established between close friends as well as between husband and wife. If during this time, a sense of intimacy is not established with a mate or friends, then Erikson believes that the person becomes isolated, without anyone to share with or care about.

GENERATIVITY VS. SELF-ABSORPTION

During middle age, people either begin to be concerned about others beyond their immediate family, with the good of society or future generations, or they become self-absorbed. Either they become actively involved with the welfare of young people or others outside themselves, or they, like Scrooge, care only about themselves and their own concerns and comforts.

INTEGRITY VS. DESPAIR

Persons reach their final stage when their major life's efforts are coming to a close and the person can now look back and reflect on his life and enjoy his grandchildren (if he has any). A sense of *integrity* arises when one can look back on one's life with satisfaction. However, the one who reflects more on missed opportunities and failures, realizing that it is now too late to start over again, generally lapses into despair.

While we know that there is so very much still to be learned about this whole process of growing up, Erikson's views do bring, I believe, a certain amount not only of helpful insight to parents, but also an awareness of the great influence of society on the development of a child. The burden for development does not rest totally on the parent, nor is there cause to despair when a child does not develop in each stage just as we would want, for Erikson always stresses the hope that failures at one stage of development may be overcome in later stages.

GROWING IN WISDOM

Let us now turn to the New Testament as we pursue this line of thinking. In the second chapter of Luke's gospel, this statement is made about our Lord's growth: "And Jesus increased, in wisdom and in stature, and in favor with God and man." (Luke 2:52). It is hard to imagine a more precise picture of a growing child. There are four basic areas of growth herein:
1. "Wisdom" which implies knowledge and how to apply it;
2. "Stature" means simply physical and chronological development;
3. "In favor with God"—a spiritual development;
4. "And man"—social development.

This is a good filter through which periodically to review and discuss our own children's growth development. In this chapter, "wisdom" and growth "in favor with God" are both concerns about which we shall think.

Wisdom means more than just knowledge and how to relate it to life's challenges. I see in wisdom the whole concept of values. Just providing our children with their physical needs is surely not enough. The story of "millionaire Dexter Coffin who did time in Gucci loafers" *(The Washington Post;* July 4, 1981) provides an example:

Dexter Coffin III was given his first outboard motorboat when he was 6, his first horse at 13, his first motorbike at 14, his first car at 16. At the age of 14, he discovered that a family trust fund paid his parents $7400 a month to provide for his needs.

He grew up believing that the world and most of the people in it existed for his amusement. 'I knew who the hired help was when I was 3 or 4 years old,' he said. 'I had the impression that the people who waited on us at various clubs, at the lawn parties, and in my house were put on earth to serve me. I figured there had to be a reason why I was receiving all these things. My conclusion was that I was special.'

Then he found out that he wasn't, that there were other teenagers who were more likely to be "successes." So he rebelled.

He started drinking and womanizing at 16, luring rich girls from Palm Beach to cheap motel rooms.

He drove a Lincoln Continental Mark III and spent a fortune on cocaine. As a yacht broker, he flew off to Europe with a buyer's money and returned home to face grand larceny charges. He was in and out of jail for seven years, once working on a road gang in state-issue dungarees and Gucci loafers.

Here's what he says about his life:

"I was given far too much, too quickly. I don't think a kid is emotionally equipped to determine what his limits should be. I felt I could do whatever I wanted to, whenever I wanted, without regard to other people. I did things without really caring if I got caught. I figured there would always be somebody to work it out for me."

Parents, he says, have to decide whether it is more important to be successful, upper-income people or to raise children in a solid, family-oriented atmosphere. "I don't think you can have both these days. . . . The values that got you the money are not the same values that you use to raise children."

More and more frequently we are hearing that growing up affluent can be a curse. In three of the most wealthy Chicago suburbs of the North Side, thirty-nine teenagers took their lives in a recent eighteen-month period. The records of these youths are so very similar: bright, hardworking, successful parents who provide magnificently for their children's material needs but are often too busy to really enter into their children's lives and help them establish their own values.

Another *Washington Post* article, "The Cost of Money," (July 4, 1981) illustrates this problem vividly. An excerpt of that article follows:

> For the minority of affluent teenagers who wash out, the seeds of failure may have been sown in infancy, according to many psychiatrists.

The breakdown begins in the first few months of a child's life, when affluent, ambitious and busy parents do not take time to establish a presence for their child that is "consistent, continuous and caring," according to Dr. Eliot Sorel, a cultural psychiatrist and assistant professor of psychiatry at George Washington University Medical School. The failure to establish that bond in infancy colors the trust that children have for their parents throughout their adolescence, Sorel says.

In Prisoners of Childhood, a new book about how narcissistic parents deform the emotional lives of their children, Swiss psychoanalyst Alice Miller writes that insecure, confused parents can strip their infants of the chance to ever develop self-confidence.

Miller says that infants have both a compelling need to be loved as simply what they are and "an amazing ability to perceive and respond intuitively" to what their parents expect of them. If an infant's parents deny him acceptance, the child will unconsciously attempt to become whatever he thinks parents expect (frequently a "good" child who never cries, gets angry, jealous or sad).

Miller, echoing the thinking of many child psychiatrists in the United States, says this can be very harmful when the child becomes an adolescent: "Understandably, these patients complain of a sense of emptiness, futility or homelessness, for the emptiness is real. A process of emptying, impoverishment and partial killing of his potential actually took place when all that was alive and spontaneous in him was cut off."

Dr. Sorel at George Washington University says this destructive parent-child relationship is nothing new, but that in the past it was partially corrected by grandparents and other members of the extended family who gave children love and acceptance. With the rapid increase in American mobility—the Census Bureau says that half of the population moves every five years—Sorel says the "correction emotional experience" offered by grandparents and other family members has fallen off sharply.

The writer, Blaine Harden, then summarizes the conclusions of various counselors about deteriorating family relationships:

Whether parents are divorced or not, psychiatrists interviewed across the country say they've seen a marked decline during the past decade in the quality of parent-child relationships among many affluent families.

"I see parents who are refusing to be parents, who refuse to stand for something or say to their kids that there is right and wrong," says Dr. Bret Burquest, president of the American Society for Adolescent Psychiatry and a child psychiatrist who treats affluent families in West Los Angeles.

"So many of the kids I work with have no specific time that they have to come home, no restrictions on their use of cars or credit cards. When there are not limits, these kids get very nervous," Burquest says.

The nervousness begins, psychiatrists say, when a child grows old enough to appreciate gifts and soon realizes that there may be no limits to what he can have. Many affluent parents assuage their guilt for not giving more of their time by buying oodles of toys.

"Children are indulged with trivia—superficial material things—and at the same time they are denied meaningful acceptance. There is no gut-level acceptance of children for what they are," says Dr. C. Gibson Dunn, a psychiatrist and medical doctor at the Springwood Psychiatric Institute in Leesburg.

The indulgence continues, Dunn says, as children become teenagers, with parents giving their kids virtually everything they want except their time and "real standards of what's good and bad."

"The kids don't have to make any hard choices between the material things they want. They don't have to earn anything. They can have it all," said Dunn, who treats many affluent teenagers from the Washington area.

He and other child psychiatrists say that troubled affluent adolescents appear as strangely hollow adults, they have grown frighteningly fast, with a razor-sharp understanding of social status, money and sex, but without the decision-making standards to control their knowledge and toys.

"Kids grow up on the 10th story, but there is no foundation beneath them," said Dunn.

By the time they become fifteen and sixteen years old, a rebellious, troubled age under the best of circumstances, many affluent kids are "overprogrammed" with athletic or cultural activities, have become a vortex of contradictory values, undisciplined impulses and an extraordinary pressure to measure up to the success of their parents, psychiatrists say.

RIGHT VERSUS WRONG

For the Christian the heart of the whole question of children and values lies with the question of right and wrong. We believe in right and wrong; how do we teach our children to know the difference? We're not just talking about passing on a list of approved behavior traits but rather the ability to reason and think through the rightness or wrongness, the fairness or unfairness of a situation. How do we help our children grow in their own ability to have wise judgment?

There are two dimensions to moral judgment: *what* you believe to be right or wrong and *why* you believe something is right or wrong. For instance, we teach, and even a wee child can understand, that honesty is right and dishonesty is wrong. It is wrong to lie. It is likely that we teach this to our children when they are quite young and they will hold to this value always, but their *reasons* may change as time goes by.

When a child is young, we teach values by punishment and reward. If the child violates the value, he or she is punished. Therefore the child learns that if he is dishonest bad things happen, but when he is honest the good things happen (obviously consistency in discipline is crucial in order to instill this early value system). But this is only the first stage in value department. (Dr. Ted Ward's book, *Values Begin at Home,* Victor, 1979, is quite helpful along this line.)

Eventually a second factor begins to exert an influence when the child moves beyond punishment/rewards thinking to realizing that being honest *pleases* mom and dad and therefore honesty is a good thing because it makes *them* happy. The child realizes that there is an external source of right and wrong and that there are those who determine the difference. Parents are usually the major influence here but the influence of other models is clearly very great also, particularly during the junior and senior high school years. Sometimes a child doesn't move out of this stage even though he has completed high school.

The third stage is where the value, or the moral, gets built into your own system. The child actually adopts the value for himself because it seems right to him. Often this process does not begin until late adolescence or into the twenties. During this phase the most important means of moral influence is dialogue, sharing your reasons for your values in conversation with your children. It is my very strong conviction, however, that unless the parent has cultivated the habit of regular caring and listening conversation with his child, he will often not be able to pull off such conversations with his teenaged or young adult child.

You can't really ensure that your adult child will behave in such and such a way; rewards and punishment no longer work and even your example may not be all that influential. But sharing from the heart and talking through an issue can have a powerful effect. One major reason why so many young people raised in Christian homes don't internalize biblical values is there has been no place for mature dialogue which looks at the "whys" behind the "whats."

HOW DOES A CHILD GROW?

If, as a child gets older, we continue to make the rules just by saying, "Dad says so" we are freezing our children into the second stage of value development and producing mere legalists. We must lay down careful and consistent laws for our children while they are small, of course, but we have found in our family that even when the children are small it is still important to discuss the "whys" behind the "whats." Not that a child shouldn't *obey* unless his parents can give him a good reason why, but one of the best things we can do, even during their early years, is to get involved in talking and thinking together about the moral actions we take.

I have wondered if this were not the problem with the sons of Samuel, the Old Testament prophet. Look at these few paragraphs from the story of this great and matchless Old Testament hero.

> Elkanah had two wives, Hannah and Peninnah. Peninnah had children, but Hannah did not (I Samuel 1:2).
>
> She was deeply distressed and prayed to the Lord, and wept bitterly. And she vowed a vow and said, "O Lord of hosts, if thou wilt indeed look on the affliction of thy maidservant, and remember me, and not forget thy maidservant, but wilt give to thy maidservant a son, then I will give him to the Lord all the days of his life, and no razor shall touch his head." . . . They rose early in the morning and worshiped before the Lord; then they went back to their house at Ramah. And Elkanah knew Hannah his wife, and the Lord remembered her; and in due time Hannah conceived and bore a son, and she called his name Samuel, for she said, "I have asked him of the Lord" (I Samuel 1:10–11, 19–20).
>
> The boy Samuel grew up in the service of the Lord (I Samuel 2:21b).
>
> The boy Samuel continued to grow and to gain favor both with the Lord and with men (I Samuel 2:26).
>
> As Samuel grew up, the Lord was with him and made come true everything that Samuel said. So all the people of Israel from one end of the country to the other, knew that Samuel was indeed a prophet of the Lord. The Lord continued to reveal himself at Shiloh, where he had appeared to Samuel and had spoken to him. And when Samuel spoke, all Israel listened (I Samuel 3:19–21).
>
> Samuel ruled Israel as long as he lived. Every year he would go around Bethel, Gilgal, and Mizpah, and in these places he would settle disputes. Then he would go back to his home in Ramah, where also he would serve as judge. In Ramah he built an altar to the Lord (I Samuel 7:15–17).
>
> When Samuel grew old, he made his sons judges in Israel. The older son was named Joel and the younger one Abijah; they were judges in Beersheba. But they did not follow their father's example;

> they were interested only in making money, so they accepted bribes and did not decide cases honestly. Then all the leaders of Israel met together, went to Samuel in Ramah, and said to him, "Look, you are getting old and your sons don't follow your example. So then, appoint a king to rule over us, so that we will have a king, as other countries have." Samuel was displeased with their request for a king. . . . (I Samuel 8:1–6a).
>
> The people paid no attention to Samuel, but said "No! We want a king, so that we will be like other nations, with our own king to rule us and to lead us out to war and to fight our battles" (I Samuel 8:19–20).

A more godly, more respected servant of God has never served, but for some reason he failed to communicate those values to his own sons and eventually the people turned their backs on him. As you read his life story you get an impression of a man who was always on the go and serving God, but you don't see him spending time with his children. Certainly they were guided through the first two stages of value development, but one wonders if Samuel ever entered into the third phase. Perhaps the problem lies with the decision of his own mother, made out of gratitude to God for a long-awaited child, to dedicate Samuel to the Lord's service whereby she took him to the old priest Eli who actually raised Samuel from the time he was seven or eight. Samuel certainly didn't learn anything from Eli about the process of value development in one's children.

> The sons of Eli were scoundrels. They paid no attention to the Lord or to the regulations concerning what the priests could demand from the people. . . . This sin of the sons of Eli was extremely serious in the Lord's sight, because they treated the offerings to the Lord with such disrespect. . . . Eli was now very old. He kept hearing about everything his sons were doing to the Israelites and that they were even sleeping with the women who worked at the entrance to the Tent of the Lord's presence. So he said to them, "Why are you doing these things? Everybody tells me about the evil you are doing. Stop it, my sons! This is an awful thing the people of the Lord are talking about! If a man sins against another man, God can defend him; but who can defend a man who sins against the Lord?" But they would not listen to their father. . . . (Samuel 2:12, 13a, 17, 22–25a).

Samuel's only model for childraising was a father who was so out of touch with his sons that his neighbors had to tell him what they were doing. When Eli finally did confront them, he could only tell them how they ought to behave. We must be careful not to read too much into the story, but it sounds as though Eli could have used a FLAG group when he was a younger father!

As children grow up, it's important for them to see their parents taking stands on moral issues in the public arena and to discuss these things in family gatherings. If the child disagrees, this is a valuable opportunity, not to explode, but to ask, "Why?" and discuss it. They need to find their own answer to these questions, so a good response is "Never mind that we disagree, just tell me why you see it that way?" Seek understanding first and *then* agreement. (More on this in a later chapter.)

MEETING AND DISCUSSION

Spend some time discussing the reading for this week and then enjoy the following study. Take twenty or so minutes to work on it alone, quietly, and then share together from your findings.

Read Luke 15:11–32. The parable of the prodigal son has more aptly been called that of the waiting father, for it is really a parable about God the Father and we the prodigal children. After prayer and previewing this passage, read it through two or three times and then reflect on the following questions:

1. Do you see any parallels between this story and the reading you did this week?

2. List every quality or characteristic of the father (note the verse in which this characteristic is found).

3. Try to explain briefly how each of these qualities is true as well of God.

4. How have you experienced each of these characteristics of God in your own relationship with Him?

5. In your relationship with *your* child(ren), are there some of these qualities which you need help in developing more fully in your life? Which ones are they?

6. How, perhaps, could the others in the group be of help to you?

7. What can *you* do to see these qualities become more developed in your life?

Pray together in closing.

CHAPTER 11

A Child's Faith and the Sacraments

Some time ago, the following statistics jumped out from the newspaper at me: "Seventy-nine percent of the teens surveyed in a Gallup Poll consider the Ten Commandments relevant guidelines for today, but only 85 percent know one or more and 35 percent, five or more. Sixty-eight percent remembered the one prohibiting stealing. More know the commandment against adultery than the one banning murder. Only 10 percent could name the one prohibiting idolatry." Young people in America don't know much about Christian teaching.

The older my children become and the more I observe other families, the more I wonder, "Why is it that some children from Christian homes apparently reject their parents' Christian faith while others do not?" What are the crucial ingredients which, when properly combined, eventually produce a mature Christian man or woman? Only God knows the answers to such questions, surely, and I expect that they differ greatly from one child to another. In this chapter, we will look at some important convictions, both doctrinal and practical, that relate to this question. Perhaps the logical place to begin is with the sacrament of Holy Baptism.

Holy Baptism is a sacred action that symbolizes a deep, hidden reality in a person's life and in his relationship with God. If the person baptized is an infant, the sacrament has one meaning. If the person baptized is an adult, the meaning is somewhat different.

But whatever the age of the one baptized, baptism is the birth rite of the worldwide Christian church. We know from our own experience that, as we pass from certain states of experience to others, some rite is often performed. An alien who becomes an American citizen participates in the rite of becoming a citizen. A civilian who joins the armed services participates in a similar rite of passage. The rite speaks both to the initiate and to the whole community.

In just the same way, when someone becomes a member of the church family, either by being born into a Christian home or by deciding for himself that he has come to believe in Christ as his Lord and wants to join the church, a definite ceremony or rite is performed. That rite is Baptism.

HISTORICAL BACKGROUND

The word "to baptize" is from the Greek word "baptizo" and means to dip, to immerse or to wash. At the time of Christ, various pagan religions utilized various forms of baptism (some using water, some using blood, and so on) to initiate their converts. It was customary among the Jews to baptize the Gentile proselytes to Judaism as well.

John the Baptist brought new meaning to the word in that he urged Baptism on the Jews as well. He called the religious leaders, as well as the common folk, to repent of their sins against God and be baptized to signify their personal repentance. In doing this they would receive God's forgiveness:

> John . . . went about into all the regions about Jordan preaching a baptism of repentance for the forgiveness of sins . . . and they were baptized by him in the river Jordan, confessing their sins (Luke 3:3–6).

Jesus commanded his disciples to baptize those who repented and accepted his Good News, and who sought to follow him:

> Go therefore and make disciples of all the nations baptizing them in the name of the Father and the Son and the Holy Spirit, teaching them to observe all that I commanded you (Matthew 28:19–20).

Jesus' disciples did indeed baptize new converts throughout their ministry. Peter said to them:

> Repent and let each of you be baptized in the name of Jesus Christ for the forgiveness of your sins and you shall receive the gift of the Holy Spirit (Acts 2:38; *see also* Acts 3:41, 8:38, 16:33).

The disciples certainly baptized adults, but they baptized whole families at a time as well (Acts 16:33, I Corinthians 1:16). This may mean that little children, as well as adults, were baptized in the earliest days of the church. We do know for certain that infant baptism was a common practice by the end of the second century.

Baptism has always been an indispensable accompaniment to conversion (unless, of course, baptism were not possible as in the case of the repentant thief on the cross). True conversion to Christ was always attested and witnessed to by the converted one's own participation in this sacrament. As the church expanded and developed in different metropolitan cities, the custom was that new converts would be instructed in the teachings of Christ until they were considered able to assume adult Christian responsibilities. Then these "catechumens" would be baptized. This was a time of great rejoicing for the Christian community. In the early church much courage was demanded of these converts, for to publicly declare oneself a Christian was often to invite severe persecution. In joyfully welcoming these new brothers and sisters in the rite of baptism, the Christians were also pledging their acceptance of mutual responsibility for the growth and nurture of these new members of Christ's Body.

WHAT DOES BAPTISM SYMBOLIZE?

Baptism is a sacramental rite (something done to symbolize an inner reality) which formally admits a candidate on the Christian church. It is an action that represents an inner spiritual birth into life in relationship to God.

Jesus taught that it was not enough for a person to be born physically, but that a person had to be born spiritually in order to be a member of the family of God: "You must be born again" (John 3:7). When a child is born, he becomes a member of a human family with earthly parents. When a person is born spiritually, he becomes a member of God's family and can call God Almighty his own "Daddy" (Romans 8:15).

There is only one way that this spiritual birth can occur and this is when, in response to God's love, a person opens up his life to God and becomes willing to live his life as God desires him to live it.

The Bible teaches that God created the whole world and mankind as well, and that God desired man to experience a joyful, fulfilling existence on the earth.

> And God created man in his own image . . . male and female. . . .
> And God blessed them and said to them, "Be fruitful and multiply and fill the earth and subdue it" (Genesis 1:27–28).

God's desire was that man should return his love and live according to God's guidelines. But from the very beginning, man did not return God's love and went his own way.

> Although they knew God they did not honor him as God or give thanks to him, but they became futile in their thinking and their senseless minds were darkened (Romans 1:21).
>
> Since all have sinned and fall short of the glory of God...." (Romans 3:23).

God sent his spokesmen and worked throughout history to call people back to himself, but the vast majority of people throughout history have simply not heeded God's call. This attitude of self-sufficient indifference to God is called sin. All of us are sinners in that all of us have, in one way or another, chosen to heed our own selfish desires rather than respond to God's call. We have all done wrong things that we ought not to have done and left undone those things which we ought to have done.

In addition, all of us have broken God's laws by actions or attitudes. The result of our sin is that we are separated from God. Once we turn our backs on God, there is only one way in which we can completely come into relationship with him and that is if he himself is willing to forgive our sins and welcome us into relationship with him. This was God's major purpose in sending his only Son into the world. He came as a revealer of God's nature and as a reconciler between God and man. Those who welcomed him were able, through him, to come into a real and new relationship with God, the kind of close relationship God had always wanted to have with us.

> But to all who received him, who believed in his name, he gave power to become children of God (John 1:12).

Those who did not welcome Christ and his message were rejecting God's most lovely, most incredible and *final* offer of reconciliation.

> He was in the world, and the world was made through him, yet the world knew him not. He came to his own home, and his own people received him not (John 1:10–11).
>
> No one who denies the Son has the Father. He who confesses the Son has the Father also (I John 2:23).
>
> In this the love of God was made manifest among us, that God sent his only Son into the world, so that we might live through him. In this is love, not that we loved God but that he loved us and sent his Son to be the propitiation for our sins (I John 4:9–10).

OUR NEED—GOD'S RESPONSE

We know that when we break a law we must suffer the consequence. This is true in any society. The Bible teaches us that when we break God's law (when we go our own way rather than God's), the punishment is spiritual *death;* that is, we are cut off from the life of God.

When we come to the point of believing God's great love for us, of sorrowing for our own sins, of wanting to turn the control of our lives over to him and of accepting Jesus Christ as his true Son, who came to reconcile us to God, then we are *born* spiritually. God forgives our sins, indwells our lives by the Holy Spirit and we begin to grow as God desires us to grow into the mature Christians he wants us to be.

Jesus once made an amazing statement:

> Behold, I stand at the door and knock; if any one hears my voice and opens the door, I will come in to him and eat with him, and he with me (Revelation 3:20).

When we ask Christ into our lives, he will come into our lives and stay with us. He restores our broken relationship with God.

It is this new birth that we celebrate and "act out" in Holy Baptism, for baptism symbolizes dying to one way of life (that is, living for anyone or anything other than God) and beginning a new way of living—living God's way.

Now the mere external rite of baptism by clergy doesn't bring about any magical change. The change occurs inside a person when, because of the Gospel and the work of the Holy Spirit, that person becomes willing to change. Baptism doesn't provide a ticket to heaven. Only Jesus can ensure our acceptance into Heaven, and he made that possible by dying for our sins on the cross. St. Paul stresses this *inner* character of the sacraments when he writes:

> For he is not a real Jew who is one outwardly, nor is true circumcision something external and physical. He is a Jew who is one inwardly, and real circumcision is a matter of the heart, spiritual and not literal (Romans 2:28–29).

What baptism does is publicly demonstrate that the person being baptized has, by God's mercy, made his decision to live for Christ and in Christ's Body.

When adults are baptized, the baptism comes *after* the fact of personal commitment to live for Christ. It is a public, sacramental demonstration of a prior fact in the same way that Elizabeth II was crowned in Westminster Abbey in June 1953, but had actually been serving as queen for some months before the public rite of coronation.

When infants are baptized, the meaning is more complicated. How can a small child, who has *no* apparent knowledge of Christ be baptized to symbolize a Christian commitment already made? He can't. Children are baptized prior to, and in anticipation of, the person's decision to follow Christ, just as adults are baptized *after* this decision.

WHY LITTLE CHILDREN?

Why do we do this? Children are God's most precious gift to parents. We know that God cares deeply for little children. We find an intense interest and concern for children in the biblical stories of Moses, Samuel, Isaiah, John, and many others. In fact, the Son of God himself became a tiny child, in order to show his care for us.

As God cares for children, so do we, and we want the very best for our children, in the spiritual realm as well as the material. You want your child, from the very first, to enter into a relationship with God that will last forever.

Now, should we shut children out of the church just because they are too young to exhibit a definitive faith in Christ? No. We bring them into the church through the entry rite of infant baptism as the beginning of their childlike relationship to God who is the Lord of their family. This is in *anticipation* of their own future adult personal decision to follow the God of their parents.

God himself initiated this concept with Abraham, the father of the Jewish people, through the rite of circumcision. From the time of Abraham on, infants were admitted as members of the Jewish community by this public act. Abraham himself was circumcised as an adult because of his faith in God, but Isaac and all Jews since have been circumcised as infants in *anticipation* of their faith. During the whole period of time from Abraham until Christ (fifteen hundred years or more), God accepted children into his family on the basis of their parents' faith. Then when the child reached an appropriate age and was taught the things of God, he made his own personal decision to follow God, and he was accepted as an adult member of the Jewish faith.

This was the recognized rule in the day of Jesus, and since he did not teach otherwise, it would be seen to apply to the Christian church as well. This is our New Testament foundation for infant baptism. It is the view that has been taken by the majority of Christians down through the ages.

Christ's attitude toward children was one of affection, concern and gentleness. He did not refuse them his blessing but purposely laid his hands in blessing on what must have been countless little ones during the years of his ministry. The significance of this cannot be overstated. They were capable of receiving the blessing no matter how young they were.

And they were bringing children to him, that he might touch them; and the disciples rebuked them. But when Jesus saw it he was indignant, and said to them, 'Let the children come to me, do not hinder them; for to such belongs the Kingdom of God. Truly, I say to you, whoever does not receive the Kingdom of God like a child shall not enter it.' And he took them in his arms and blessed them, laying his hands upon them (Mark 10:13–16).

In the Book of Acts, there are two prominent stories of entire families being baptized in the early church.

"And when she was baptized, with her household, she besought us, saying, 'If you have judged me to be faithful to the Lord, come to my house and stay.' And she prevailed upon us" (Acts 16:15).

And they said, "Believe in the Lord Jesus, and you will be saved, you and your household" (Acts 16:31).

And he took them the same hour of the night, and washed their wounds, and he was baptized at once, with all his family (Acts 16:33).

St. Paul addresses little children in Christian families in such a way as to suggest that they are already included in the church.

Children, obey your parents in the Lord, for this is right (Ephesians 6:1).

Children, obey your parents in everything, for this pleases the Lord (Colossians 3:20).

For the unbelieving husband is consecrated through his wife, and the unbelieving wife is consecrated through her husband. Otherwise, your children would be unclean, but as it is they are holy (I Corinthians 7:14).

LIKE PLANTING A SEED

Baptism for an infant is like the planting of a seed in good soil. It is an action performed in faith that one day, what is now being begun by the parents, will be completed by the child himself. God forbid that a child be baptized when the parents themselves are not professed Christians. It is not reasonable to expect that parents who make no profession of Christianity could bring their children up as Christians and lead them to an adult personal decision for Christ.

Christian parents present their child before the church, dedicating themselves to the Christian nurture of the child and dedicating the child to God. The church gathered accepts the infant as a new member and acknowledges its own responsibility to help in the Christian nurture of the child.

The roads which different children move along in coming to adult Christian faith are very different for different individuals. Both my wife and I were raised in deeply committed and loving Christian, Episcopalian homes. I can never remember a time when I did not have a strong faith in Christ and a close relationship with him. My wife, however, in a very similar home, grew up somehow without the assurance of that close relationship with Christ. She says that she did not become a Christian until she made a personal, adult decision at age twenty-one to invite Jesus Christ into her life to be her Master and Savior. She had gone to church, prayed, and even taught Sunday school, but the certainty of knowing Jesus personally was not there.

Your children will travel different roads. When they are sprinkled with water and marked with the sign of the cross, that is but the beginning. Baptism in no way guarantees that the child will grow up to be a believing Christian. However, it is the first step and we are privileged to be able to take that step.

As a parent, your number-one responsibility is to be certain, in your own mind, that your own relationship with God is as it should and can be.

As we have seen, successful parenting is very difficult in our age and culture. We need all the help we can get.

The Lord Jesus stands ready to come into our lives and give us the strength and wisdom we need to be the parents we should want to be. Most likely your children have already been baptized, but it will be a worthwhile exercise to pull out your Prayer Book and read through the service again. As you meditate on these things, you may want to make the following prayer your own:

> Dear God, I thank you for my child, which you have enabled me to have. I thank you for the love you have for me, as well as my precious child. I need your help. I have turned too often from you and pursued my own ways. I confess my sins and gratefully receive your forgiveness. I open the door of my life and ask your Son Jesus to come in and be with me to guide me and strengthen me as a parent and as a Christian. I want to be the person and parent that you have created me to be. These things I pray through Jesus Christ, our Lord. Amen.

THOSE CRUCIAL YEARS

During the years following baptism, the child grows in all the ways we have already discussed. He will grow in his relationship with the Lord as well, we hope and pray. Much of the rest of this workbook is directed to things we, as parents, can do to aid in this process of spiritual growth.

Some parents feel that by participating in church school, their child receives all the specifically Christian teaching he needs. You know better than that or you wouldn't be in this FLAG group. The amount of time that church school teachers have with the typical Episcopalian child is infinitesimal; probably no more than 1 percent of the child's time is spent in a church school class. A wise Sunday school teacher attempts to teach the Bible and its relevance to his or her students, but realizes that the more lasting influence will most likely be as a friend and particularly as a model for the child. I expect that my third grader will long remember his rugby-playing, soccer-enthusiast Sunday school teacher, because of his joyous enthusiasm for Christ, for life, and for sport more than for his expositions on the parables! I don't remember a thing that Mrs. Redding taught me during the two years I had her as a church school teacher, but I'll never forget how her faith in the Lord sustained her when her son was killed in a freak accident.

Surely some Sunday school teachers are able to really teach certain aspects of the faith to our children, but that responsibility is largely ours, and therefore family prayers, family Bible study, and family discussions about the whole, vast scope of life and what it means to be a Christian must be an integral part of our children's growing-up years. Commitment to Christ must be a progressive thing that matures all the way to the grave and beyond. It is my conviction that a five-year-old can love Jesus sincerely and be as obedient to what he or she understands of Jesus' demands for discipleship as can a fifty-year-old Christian leader. But as the child grows older, he must continue to make reaffirmation of his commitment to Christ as his horizons, his abilities, his opportunities, and his temptations ever broaden.

For this reason, we are encouraging two further points of public Christian affirmation for young people in our own parish: admission to Holy Communion and to confirmation. For many years, these two events were synonymous, but no more. When a child and the child's parents both feel that it is time to give serious thought to receiving Holy Communion, we use that occasion as an opportunity to meet with both the children and the parents on successive Saturday mornings to do two things: Review the Service of Holy Eucharist in detail, analyzing each element; and talk with the children about what it means to invite Jesus to be King of their lives. Twice a year, we have children in grades 3–6, and sometimes older, participate in the classes which culminate generally at Easter or Christmas when the children receive the sacrament for the first time. Our aim in this class is to help the children affirm for themselves, publicly, their desire to be committed Christians.

Confirmation is no longer a standard sixth-grade ritual, but has been put off until a child is in high school to stress that in confirmation a young person, on the verge of adulthood, is now not only reaffirming his or her loyalty to Christ, already expressed at the time when he or she was admitted to Holy Communion, but is committing himself or herself to assume adult responsibilities as a lay minister of Christ.

These events, Baptism, admission to Holy Communion, and confirmation, will almost always have abiding significance for the child only if, in the life of the family, there is an ongoing experience of the reality of Christ. One of the great tragedies throughout the history of God's people is the consistent pattern by which the children or grandchildren of committed Christians seem to fall away from the faith and values of their parents.

King David was deeply committed to the Lord. His son Solomon started out in his father's footsteps but eventually compromised his morality and his faith. David's grandson, Rehoboam, completely abandoned the Lord. Over and over in the Bible we see examples of godly parents—Noah, Abraham, Samuel, among others—whose descendants turned away from the Lord.

We see this pattern in the nation of Israel over and over again as well. During the lifetime and leadership, for instance, of Joshua, the people of Israel followed him in his example of strong commitment to the Lord (Joshua 24:14 ff.). Those elders who were his contemporaries and who outlived Joshua knew the Lord and the ways of the Lord (Joshua 2:7 ff.). But the next generation fell away (Judges 2:10–11).

The same pattern seems to be true of churches, Christian schools and other Christian institutions. A school begun by sincere, godly Christian folk, based upon a strong commitment to orthodox Christian principles, usually within forty to sixty years becomes rather secularized, although it may still retain the outward trappings of the religion of its founders.

I have noted a pattern among families in the South. The old generation—those now in their eighties or nineties—often hold tenaciously to deep faith in Christ and to biblical truth and virtues, and are concerned about people and in love with Christ. Their children—now in their fifties or sixties—grew up in the atmosphere, believed what their parents taught them, remained in the church, kept true to the values of their parents, but had somehow lost or never found the fire or vitality in a personal relationship with Jesus Christ. And so, although they maintained a strong involvement in the church and outward veneer of Christian morality, because there was no vital link with Christ personally, they exemplified a sort of superficial Christianity. *Their* children—now in their twenties and thirties—were quick to spot the hypocrisy and superficiality of their parents' brand of Christianity and therefore rejected the whole thing, deserting the church and the faith.

I believe that this pattern is not unique to the people of the late nineteenth and twentieth centuries. This three-fold stage of decline has always been a problem. Generation A has Christ, B has the church but not Christ, and generation C doesn't really care. This ultimately leads either to a sort of spiritual extinction *or* to a rediscovering of the reality of Christ as we saw in the Jesus movement of the 1970's. Those kids discovered Christ, returned to the churches with newfound faith and true piety, and now are raising families of their own. The need, now, is to pass on to our children the genuine article of Christianity rather than simply passing on a commitment to the *outward* trappings of faith.

We can do this only if we pray for our children, if we talk with our children, if we help them to come to know the Lord personally, and if we stay in close relationship with them all along the way so as to help them grow into Christian maturity. In the following chapters, we will consider some thoughts as to how to do this.

Please walk through the following Bible study in preparation for your next meeting.

BIBLE STUDY

Complete the following Bible Study for your next meeting: Read the following accounts of two sets of parents who so longed to have children. Please note your answers in writing.

Genesis 17:15–21
Genesis 21:1–7
Genesis 22:1–19
I Samuel 1:1–28

1. What similarities do you see in these two stories?

2. In I Samuel 1:28 what is the meaning of "dedicating" a child to the Lord? How did Abraham demonstrate that he had dedicated his child to the Lord?

3. When is it appropriate to dedicate one's child to the Lord?

4. What became of Isaac and Samuel? Did they live up to their parents' expectations?

5. "Train up a child in the way he should go and when he is old, he will not depart from it" (Proverbs 22:6). What is the meaning of "the

way he should go?" Does it imply a certain career? (Look at various translations.)

6. Parents sometimes overzealously (or *under* zealously) seek to influence their child's thinking about future career. Can you share any examples you have known? What are the dangers?

7. How then can we most helpfully aid our children in their planning and preparation for their professions/careers?

8. Look at John 6:29, John 15:4-5, Galatians 5:22-23, and Luke 6:40. What do you think God wants our children to become? Is His main concern for them, their individual accomplishments or their character? How does I Corinthians 12:4-11 (and following) relate to all of this?

MEETING AND DISCUSSION

1. What things did you find helpful in the reading this week?

2. Can you relate personal experiences from your own life or from the experience of your own children or others whom you know, in which baptism, confirmation or admission to Holy Communion have been especially meaningful?

3. Do you have any suggestions for any in the group whose child(ren) will be involved soon in one of these three events?

4. Spend some time discussing your reflection on the Bible study questions.

5. Share any concerns for prayer.

CHAPTER 12

Family Times and Family Nights Holidays and Holy Days

Several years ago a seminary professor told me of two studies dealing with the question of the amount of time families spend together. One family counselor found that the average family with which he was in contact spent only about thirty minutes a week in serious discussions of any sort. While another report found that among successful, executive men, the fathers surveyed spent on the average only about seventeen seconds a day in meaningful conversation with each child. If these studies were accurate, the findings are, to me, alarming. It may be that this is indeed the case in many of our homes today.

A story told by Marion Jacobsen rings only too true of so many families and touches some of us in a very tender spot.

> A well-dressed couple confronted a salesgirl in a toy shop with a request for toys that would keep their children entertained. "My husband and I are both employed," explained the mother, "and the children are alone a great deal."
>
> The salesgirl showed them a variety of games and play equipment, but to each there was some objection. "It seems to me," the mother finally said impatiently, "that if you knew what we are looking for, you could find it among all these toys."
>
> The salesgirl hesitated, and then said quietly, "I'm sorry, madam. I think that what you are *really* looking for—and what your children want—is a mother and father. And we don't sell *those* here." (*How to Keep Your Family Together and Still Have Fun*; Zondervan, 1969; p. 17)

Our children don't expect us to be perfect parents. They just want us to be with them and love them. If we don't begin to spend significant time with them when they are still young, by the time we wise up, they may no longer care. You cannot program good times of communication with a child, but if you are available to your child and make a priority of spending time together, good conversations will come. "According to family therapists Carole Owens and Robert P. Jardin, symptoms of a troubled family include lack of communication, poor conflict resolution, unclear rules and expectations, avoidance of responsibility, conflict and competition between parents, lack of individual privacy and lack of respect. Conversely, the cures to these problems are found in spending fun times together, having family "meetings," establishing rules and punishments, clarifying roles and responsibilities, learning how to disagree yet support each other, giving freedom within boundaries and growing in respect for the abilities and progress of each individual in the family." (Quoted from *Parade Magazine* in *Dads Only,* February 1982.) Many parents try to set objectives, such as spending one hour a week completely alone with each child doing what the child wants to do, or taking one child out to breakfast or on a "date" or special outing every week. A wise parent will take his children to visit his place of work so that the child knows what his parent does during his working hours, and he will also visit his child's school and playground and other places where the child spends times so that he can better know about his child's own world.

MEALTIMES

Mealtimes ought to be good times of family communication as well since, particularly at suppertime, it is natural for everyone to share about their day. We will discuss this question of how to talk to your children more completely later. In this chapter, we want to think particularly about the value of making a long-term commitment to certain ongoing traditions that will improve the quality of family communication.

We have found having breakfast together as a family is quite important in that it draws us all together at the opening of the day, enabling us to keep abreast of each other's planned activities. It also provides a regular time for prayer and Bible study reading together.

When our oldest was about three, we began reading *Little Visits with God* each morning after breakfast. This is not a book of Bible stories, but of brief stories about children and the typical sorts of things that happen to little ones. Each chapter contains a clear principle of Christian living and also has questions at the end which are brief but, at the same time, help the child to reflect upon the point being stressed. As the children have grown older, we have read a great variety of children's devotional books, as well as Bible story books. With the younger ones, colorful pictures, simple wording and questions at the end of each story are quite helpful. We have discovered an excellent series of story books about Bible heroes, written by Ethel Barrett, which our children love. (See book list in appendix.)

The point of these family devotional times is not just to teach Bible stories, although that is important. What we are seeking to do is to help all the family reflect on the way God thinks and the way God wants us to think—the way God has acted in history and the ways in which we can expect Him to act in our own day. The more we can all interact in these discussions, the better. Children need to see how God's word relates to Mom's and Dad's lives as well.

We always conclude these times with prayer. We believe in a balance between extemporaneous prayers and formal memorized prayers. The prayer that we all close with is as follows:

> Good Morning, dear Lord,
> This is your day.
> I am your child;
> Please show me your way.

Before praying we think aloud about the situations before us that we need to remember in prayer, and we always pray for at least one person on the photo-covered bulletin board on the wall in our kitchen. Each day is someone's "day" to pray, although usually several chime in.

These times at breakfast become quite precious and from time to time lead into significant discussions. At other times there is hardly time to speak before the kids are off to the school bus. The time is always limited and sometimes I am away at a breakfast meeting somewhere, but the tradition becomes quite important so that the children never let us forget.

None of us wants to force our faith on our children. We want, rather, for them to come to a personal commitment of their very own in their own time. But we want them also to see that life lived in relationship with the Lord is completely natural, and that he is interested in the totality of our lives. Therefore we must always be willing to stop whatever we are doing and listen to our child's concerns and then, if appropriate, pray with them about it—whether it is a cut on the finger or a fear about that day's baseball game or social studies' quiz.

The following thoughts on prayers are from Elva Anson.

"Under the Spreading Grapefruit Tree" is a delightful story about a father who tried to help God out when his six-year-old daughter asked, "If you pray really hard, God can do anything. Right, Daddy?"

The child planted a grapefruit seed. She prayed that God would cause her seed to grow into a grapefruit tree by Christmas, which was four days away. The father tried to reason with his little girl, but she said firmly, "I asked God, and God can do anything."

The father explained that God had rules for growing things and one of these rules was that seeds grow slowly. "You don't expect God to change His rules just for you, do you?" asked the father.

The little girl said that her Sunday school teacher told her that God could do anything if you prayed and had enough faith. And she was sure the seed would become a grapefruit tree by Christmas.

The father finally gave up talking, but on Christmas morning a sturdy little grapefruit tree stood in the girl's can. Her father had put it there.

The little girl took her tree to show to a friend. She came home with a bug named Horace. She had traded the tree for him. "You see, Daddy," she said excitedly, "God does answer prayer when you have faith. Now I want Horace to have bug puppies on New Year's Day, and I'm going to pray real hard."

Parents often stand helplessly by, wondering if their children's faith will be shattered when a request is not granted. This happened at our house when Janee brought a male hamster home to stay with her female. She hoped to raise young hamsters. We warned her that the venture might be unsuccessful, but she soon insisted that Scamper was pregnant.

Janee followed the instructions in her hamster book and kept the cage covered during the gestation period and for a couple of weeks afterward. When the time came for the babies to be born, Janee insisted that they were there.

She said, "I know Scamper had babies because I prayed that she would. You know God answers prayer, Mom."

When it was safe to take a look at the babies, I could see by Janee's look of horrified disbelief as she lifted the towel that no babies had been born.

Janee could not understand it. She burst into tears. "How could this happen, Mama?" she sobbed. "I asked God to let her get pregnant, and I really believed that she was. Why didn't God answer my prayer?"

Janee's dilemma is one that every Christian has to face. My answer could not be glib or superficial. There had been times in my life when I had bitterly asked the same question.

I told Janee that her experience was very difficult to understand. Sometimes God does not grant our requests, and we cannot know why. To write it off simply as God's will does not help us to feel better. I suggested she might be at a growing stage in her Christian life when God could trust her to learn a truth that would make her life more mature. He might be testing her to see if her faith in Him was based on His granting every request she made.

Janee did not get over this traumatic challenge to her faith in a few minutes or hours. It took some time before she could continue to unquestioningly serve a God she felt had disappointed her. But when the understanding and insight came, Janee's Christian maturity took a giant step forward. She no longer had the naive, unquestioning faith of a tiny child. She now trusted God in spite of circumstances. I think, too, that she realized that as humans we have put a great deal of emphasis on material things, while God is concerned with spiritual matters as well.

Trust your children to learn from their experiences. To try to protect them from hurts and disappointments will deny them the right to grow and mature. Faith can stand any test. Truth can face any challenge, and God is truth. Guide your children, but do not try to play God. That is the best way to stay out of hot water. ("Helping Faith Grow" in *Family Life Today* magazine, April, 1977; pp. 11-13. Used with permission.)

There is no limit to the creative ways in which families can learn from the Bible. When I was growing up we used to always choose from a dog-eared box of little, colored cards, a "precious promise" for the day (a card with a Bible verse on it). Then everyone would try to guess where the verse was from in the Bible. There are innumerable Bible games and fine Christian storybooks that are appropriate for reading at mealtimes.

Sometime back I discovered an amazing new children's Bible in which the entire Bible had been reduced to comic book form. (Originally this came out in a series of small paperback volumes, but now is available in one large bound book.) I gave this to my son on his seventh birthday and was totally unprepared for his response. Night after night, he sat up reading it; he finished it in a matter of days and continues to reread it. It is not unusual for him to prop up in bed and read it even on a Saturday morning when all the others are watching cartoons on TV. The amount of Bible content he has absorbed is astonishing. This book, though expensive, is well worth the investment. It is entitled *The Picture Bible* and is currently published by David C. Cook.

BEDTIME

If you have as many children as we have, bedtime can be an ordeal. But as the children get older, it can become a sweeter time. Whenever possible, we read stories to the children at bedtime. Usually these are all sorts of books—not necessarily Christian in orientation. One of our major objectives has been to develop in our children a love for reading, and the best way to do this is to read aloud to them from interesting, exciting and well-written books. At this particular moment, I am reading *Wild Bill Hickock* with one child, *The Chronicles of Narnia* (C.S. Lewis) with another, and *Tales of King Arthur* with another. *Honey for a Child's Heart* by Gladys Hunt (Zondervan; 1969) should be in every family's library because it gives a marvelous accounting of the very finest books written for children.

Bedtime often becomes an opportunity for meaningful discussions. Children rarely want to go to sleep at night and are often more inclined to share their thoughts then than at any other time. Lying on the bed and talking quietly for ten minutes or so is a wise investment in the relationship between parent and child that will result in the dividends of a closer attachment years down the line. Prayers at bedtime seem to fit naturally into this go-to-bed ritual and can be particularly meaningful if they arise out of a good conversation. We don't adhere to any sort of memorized bedtime prayer but rather vary these prayers. Sometimes we focus our bedtime prayers on thanksgiving first, then confession, then intercession. Often we just talk to the Lord in no particular order. Sometimes both the parent and child should pray, sometimes just the child. Sometimes it is fitting for only the parent to pray. On many occasions if all the children are going to bed at the same time, it is good to draw all the family together for family bedtime prayers.

FAMILY NIGHTS

Over the past several years, there has been a growing tradition in our family and in many others known as "family nights." If our schedule were not so incredibly full, it would not be necessary to set aside such evenings, but in my opinion, the practice of blocking out one night-a-week in which all the family will be at home together and involved in joint activities is quite helpful. For many years we maintained Tuesday nights as our family night, now it's Thursday. There is no regular format of events, except that on Thursdays I try to arrive home from work a little earlier so that we can have supper earlier than usual. This gives more time between supper and bedtime. The object of a family night is to do enjoyable things as a family that will enhance our communication. The possibilities are endless. Sometimes we play crazy games, sometimes we watch family movies and pop popcorn, sometimes we go on hikes or picnics or special outings to places of interest. A large and cozy fire on a cold night is often a family-night request. Sometimes I will choose a concept for the evening, or a principle, and think through various ways of communicating the meaning and importance of such concepts as the love of God or compassion or persistence.

In our home the responsibility for planning and leading family nights has always been dad's rather than mom's. In our case, mom would probably do better at it than I, but because in most families the mother generally does the majority of the organizing of the family activities, we felt that it would be better for family nights to be dad's responsibility. Often on a family night we will take some time to read or, even better, put on dress-ups and act out a Bible story. A monthly Christian magazine, *Family Life Today,* contains a helpful section of suggestions for family-night activities which can stimulate your own creative juices. I find that it usually takes me less than half an hour to decide what we will do and plan the activities.

Here are some suggested outlines (copyright *Family Life Today,* Pasadena, California. Reprinted by permission).

TALKING IS MORE THAN WORDS

For Parents:

This family time will help your family think and talk about the importance of communicating with one another. Each activity zeroes in on some factor involved in getting your message across to the other person.

ACTIVITIES FOR FAMILY TIME

SILENCE!

Help your children get a feeling about the importance of being able to talk with one another by having a time of "no talking." Rules: From the signal for *silence* until the signal to *go ahead and talk* no one can speak. All communication must be by a smile, a gesture or some form of sign language.

In less than 15 minutes your entire family will be wanting the luxury of using words!

SCRAMBLED VERSE

Make copies of the following scrambled verse for each family member: ATIMET OBEQUIET AT IME TOS PEA KUP. (Unscrambled: "A time to be quiet, a time to speak up," Ecclesiastes 3:7).

When you have unscrambled the verse, discuss it. What does it mean?

Use the following sample situations to help you talk about when it is a good time to speak up; when it is best to be quiet. Talk together about what you should say or not say in each of the following situations. Then work as a family to memorize Ecclesiastes 3:7b.

1. Your mother tells you to do something.
2. Dad asks you a question.
3. Your friend comes over to show you a new bike.
4. You don't understand a part of what the teacher said.
5. You see someone scratching up a car in the school parking lot.

WRITE A LETTER

Talk together about how a letter is a good way to "talk" with a family member who is not close by. Choose a relative, maybe a grandparent, aunt or uncle, and write a family letter.

Locate a large envelope so everyone in the family can send some kind of a message!

You can have fun with "shelf paper stationery" if you assign a portion to each member of the family. Young ones can draw pictures. Encourage school age children to also tell about their school, church activities, pets, friends, etc.

When the letter is ready, see who can think of something interesting to enclose. Maybe a leaf from your autumn tree or a family snapshot.

PUPPET CONVERSATION

Make two "sock" puppets or use puppets that you have and act out two kinds of conversations.

Conversation #1: Everyone talks and no one listens.

Conversation #2: Everyone takes turns talking and listening.

Have two family members work together to plan each puppet conversation. When the performances are over talk about which kind of conversation is best. Also decide what Ecclesiastes 3:7 says that is important in any conversation.

WORDS CAN MAKE FRIENDS

Get each person to think about how he feels when someone says "I like you."

Encourage each person to make someone else feel the same way by saying "I like you," or some other friendly word!

KINDS OF WORDS

Make a words poster that gives one-word descriptions of as many kinds of words as you can think of. Get ideas by reading Proverbs 12:18; 15:4; 16:24; 18:4; 25:15; 27:17.

PRAYER WORDS

As a family write a prayer of thanks to God for the ability to talk and communicate thoughts to one another. Give everyone in the family the opportunity to suggest a sentence for the prayer.

IF YOU HAVE TEENAGERS OR OLDER CHILDREN

In addition to activities you have chosen for family night, set aside an evening for a good time with just your older children. Take them out to dinner at a place they enjoy. Have fun talking. As the evening progresses— and it is appropriate—ask your older children's ideas on ways to improve communication in your family. Listen to their ideas with interest. Don't belittle or criticize. Your whole family may benefit from their suggestions.

IF YOU HAVE YOUNG CHILDREN
(7 years or younger)

Plan for some "undivided attention" time to spend with the youngest members of your family. Make this a time of talking with the child and listening to what he says. Maybe you will want to plan a treat. How about a hamburger and shake together, if that is your child's favorite?

LISTENING IS FUN

For Parents:

Listening is a crucial ingredient in good communication. Parents need to be examples of good listeners. For example, do you hear your children through, even when you disagree? Are you sensitive enough to listen behind your children's words to what they really mean?

During this family time your family members will have opportunities to sharpen listening skills.

ACTIVITIES FOR FAMILY TIME

CONCENTRATE

Tell family members that you are going to play a listening game that takes concentration. Have one person stand in the center of the room. He walks up to another family member, touches a part of his own body and says, "This is my leg" (or foot, finger, head, etc) as he points to a part *different* from one he has named, such as his eye. The person he is standing before must point to whatever has been named, in the case above, the leg, and identify it correctly by saying "This is my leg," before the leader counts to ten.

If he fails the listening test before the count of ten, he replaces the one in the center.

LISTEN, LISTEN, LISTEN

Read the three following Bible verses that talk about listening: James 1:19; Proverbs 21:11 and 18:13. (Read in more than one version if possible.)

What three things about listening do you discover in these verses? Can the family think of three real life examples from home, school or work that show how the three listening principles work?

THE LONGEST MINUTE

Give each family member, in turn, the opportunity to talk for one minute straight. After a family member has completed his one-minute "speech" the rest of the family should tell him what they think he said. The person who did the one-minute "talk" then tells the family what he really said. Compare views. Is there any difference? Is it easy to listen and really hear?

EARS FOR LISTENING

Cut three large ear shapes from construction paper. On each ear letter one of the following questions:

1. How do you feel when you know someone who is not really listening to you?
2. How do you think someone else feels when he knows that you are not really listening to what he says?
3. Do you ever wish someone would listen to you and really understand what you are saying?

After the family has read and discussed each question, talk about ways a person can become a more understanding listener. (Be sure to listen and try to understand the other fellow's ideas!)

LISTENING EXPERIMENT

Preparation: Before the "listening experiment," letter on slips of paper the following phrases and the voice to use: "Stop that!" (kind voice); "Stop that!" (angry voice); "Stop that!" (scared voice); "Time to get up!" (angry voice); "Time to get up!" (happy voice); "Time to get up!" (uninterested voice); "Hurry up!" (mean voice); "Hurry up!" (gentle voice); "Hurry up!" (disgusted voice).

Procedure: Have family sit in a circle. Everyone draws a slip of paper and keeps it a secret. Then, going around the circle, each person says the words on his paper using the voice suggested. Family members tell what kind of voice each one has heard.

After everyone has a turn, discuss: Which is most important in communicating feelings—what you say or how you say it?

IF YOU HAVE TEENAGERS OR OLDER CHILDREN

Make copies of the following "test" for each older child and each parent. Then take a chunk of time for parents and older children to take the test. After completing it share the results. Share honestly how you think listening in your family can be improved.

1. Do you wait until parent/teen is through talking before having your say?
2. Do you respect parent/teen opinions?
3. When parent/teen talks do you pretend that you're listening when you're not?
4. When parent/teen talks do you let your own opinions screen out what the other person is saying?
5. When parent/teen talks do you really listen or are you thinking about what you are going to say when he/she is through?

IF YOU HAVE YOUNG CHILDREN
(7 years or younger)

LISTEN, LISTEN . . .

Take a "listening walk" with your child. Be quiet and listen as you walk. Then talk about what you hear. A bird singing? A truck going by? A fire engine siren? The wind?

Take a walk through the house and listen. What can you hear? The telephone ringing? Washing machine? Someone talking?

Talk with your child about how great God is to make our ears so we can hear. Learn the Bible words: "Let everyone be quick to hear" (Jas 1:19, NASB). Pray and thank God for being able to hear.

TALKING TO GOD

For Parents:

This family time will help your family discover good ways to talk with God in prayer.

ACTIVITIES FOR FAMILY TIME

WHEN OUR FAMILY PRAYS

Talk about times when your family can remember praying together. Perhaps you will include: mealtime prayers; evening prayers; a special prayertime before leaving on a trip; prayer for a sick one in the family; etc.

Read Matthew 18:19–20 and discover who is *always* with your family when you pray.

WHAT CAN PEOPLE PRAY ABOUT?

Divide the family into two teams. Give each team a sheet of poster board, a stack of old magazines that can be cut, scissors and paste. Then ask each team to read Philippians 4:4–7 and to make a poster from letters, words and pictures cut from the magazines.

Each team's poster is to show one of the following three things: What God wants you to pray about. Or, what happens to you when you pray. Or, how these verses make you feel.

FIND THE ANSWER

What do the following bible verses say about prayer?
1. Jesus said not to pray like them. Read Matthew 6:5.
2. The kind of man whose prayer has great power. Read James 5:16.
3. Three words that tell us how to pray. Read Thessalonians 5:17.
4. Two words that Jesus prayed which show his attitude toward prayer. Read Matthew 26:42.

(Answers: Hypocrites, Righteous. Pray without ceasing. Thy will.)

GAME TIME

Have the youngest and oldest member of the family choose a game for the family to play together. Or would everyone enjoy a joke- and riddle-telling time?

THANKS FOR OUR FAMILY!

Appoint one member of the family to be the letter writer. Then have everyone in the family suggest one sentence for a prayer-thank-you-letter that thanks God for the good times your family has together. Can you also thank Him for some of the difficult times? What good things happen when the going is rough? See James 1:2-4.

IF YOU HAVE TEENAGERS OR OLDER CHILDREN

Praying will have new meaning for your older children when they discover for themselves answers to the questions, "Why pray?"

BIBLE SEARCH

Why pray? What does God's Word say? (See 1 Chron. 16:11; Matt. 7:7; 26:41; Luke 18:1; John 16:24; Eph. 6:18; Phil. 4:6; 1 Thess. 5:17).

Why pray? Who is going to answer? (See Ps. 91:15; Isa. 58:9; 65:24; John 15:7.)

IF YOU HAVE YOUNG CHILDREN
(7 years or younger)

You can help your young child learn to talk to God by praying with him. Encourage your youngster to talk to God about what has happened during the day, thanking God for friends and fun and food. Many times it helps to have a prayer that you both know to share together. Use the following poems or write prayer poems of your own.

BEDTIME PRAYER

Thank you, God, for quiet night; Give me sleep 'til morning light.
Thank you for my family; Thank you, God, for loving me.
In Jesus' name, I pray. Amen.

MEALTIME THANKS

Thank you, God, for food and drink.
For all these things so good. Thank you, God.
For those who help to grow and cook my food.

ONE FAMILY'S EXPERIENCE

One family's experience with times together, such as I have been describing, is described in the following article which I find quite encouraging.

> My family was falling apart at the seams when we first started having family times. We each had our own interests and were pursuing our own activities. I was probably the most guilty.
>
> Then at a couples' retreat conducted by family life specialist Wayne Rickerson, Barbara and I were introduced to the concept of weekly husband-wife together times. We decided that we needed them to rebuild and strengthen our marriage.
>
> The results were such a blessing that we decided to try weekly family times as well.
>
> What is a family time? It is one night a week reserved for the family. Each family member must be committed to being available at the time and date appointed. It may not be easy; it will require rescheduling of other activities or even dropping some, but it is a sacrifice that is well worth the effort.
>
> Once the family has decided *to have* family times, the next step is to determine *when* you will have family times. Having them on the same night each week is a simple method, but it may not be practical for your family.
>
> Setting aside a different night each week requires discipline, but it can be done. You just need to be sure to schedule family times *before* the week begins and before everything else fills up your calendar. Our family has used this second method for two-and-a-half years and has only missed having them two out of about 130 weeks.
>
> On school nights our family times usually run an hour. When there is no school the next day they will last as long as three or four hours.
>
> When we first tried having family times, we floundered and almost gave up. One problem was the ages of our children—two boys, 12 and 13, and a 4-year-old daughter. The boys were at an age when sitting down with parents and little sister was a bore. "Is it over yet?" they'd typically comment, soon after we had begun.
>
> And it is very difficult to plan activities which are stimulating for older children yet not beyond the capacity of younger children. Because of these problems we were tempted to give up, but we stuck with it and the Lord has blessed our family.
>
> Soon the boys began to look forward to our family times. Now if we forget to schedule them, they are quick to remind us about our omission.

Why the change in their attitudes? Because our family times have developed to suit the needs and interests of our family. Wayne Rickerson contends that each family that continues to have family times will end up with those that are best suited to them and are a little different from every other family's.

How did ours develop? As a brand new Christian, I was uneasy with prayer and unfamiliar with devotions. Therefore, our first few family times had little to do with the Christian faith. We would get together and talk, play a game, and have some dessert. This took about an hour.

Soon Barbara began sharing a verse that she had read during the week or would write out verses on cards, cut up the cards and place the pieces in an envelope and see who could reconstruct the verse most quickly.

As time went on I started opening our family times with prayer; soon we added the reading of a couple of Bible verses. Then we selected a book of the Bible to read aloud together and discuss what the verses meant to us. Before long we had developed a prayer list which we continue to review each week to see how God has answered our prayers.

We now also include a discussion time—a special time for giving praise for jobs well done (chores, school, etc.), pointing out areas that need improvement or correction, considering family decisions (how to cut expenses, etc.) and reviewing each person's schedule for the coming week.

Next we participate together in some activity. Table games are popular, with our daughter teaming up as Mom or Dad's partner so that she can be involved without slowing things down too much for the boys. Her favorite—and one the boys tolerate because we give prizes (gum, comic books, etc.) is bingo.

Other activities include going to the library, a family-oriented movie or an athletic event; going bowling, out to dinner or for ice cream—or visiting someone in the hospital. Or we will stay home to watch an especially good TV program, complete with popcorn. We've also discovered that we can check out a movie projector, 8-millimeter films or cassettes of old radio programs from the library.

You may be thinking that between the activities and the desserts that family times can get a little expensive. They can, but the expense is well worth it from our perspective. We used to do a lot of entertaining, and we never spared expense when we had company. We feel our children are even more important than company and we demonstrate this to them by treating them like they're special. We have cut out some of our individual activities and most of our entertaining in order to have quality family times together.

Besides the fun that we have together, there are some significant benefits derived from family times. We used to have real problems communicating with our boys. Except for meals they would spend most of their time at home in their rooms. Now they are eager to talk to us and on most days begin to tell me about their day the minute I walk in the door after a day at the office. And they do the same with their mother when they get home from school.

I feel that because they have been given a chance to talk freely during our family times and have found out that we are interested in what they have to say, they feel comfortable talking to us.

Another benefit is that our mealtimes are vastly improved. Because the boys used to spend so much time in their rooms, the only time we could talk to them and scold them for not doing chores, etc. was at the dinner table. Our meals were times of constant tension, pressure, and shouting.

Now we calmly discuss problems during family times. A new family policy that has worked well is that we will not discuss any controversial topic that could start an argument during mealtime. We now have pleasant mealtimes with discussions about what we have each done that day.

We have had to work at making our family times successful. It has cost us time, money, and personal sacrifice. But the blessings have far outweighed the costs. We have gotten to know one another better and have been drawn closer to each other and the Lord. And Barbara and I have been able to communicate Christian values to our children. Those rewards make any cost well worth the effort (Copyright *Family Life Today,* Pasadena, California. Reprinted by permission.)

HOLIDAYS OR HOLY DAYS

Many of our major Holidays (Thanksgiving, Easter, Christmas) are religious in origin, having initially been Holy Days, but now have been largely secularized in America. Liturgically oriented churches, like our own Episcopal church, have a strong tradition of celebrating Holy Days within the worshipping community all year round.

When God called the Jewish nation into being, He instituted the concept of Holy Days and directed that these days be celebrated together as a family. One such example is found in Exodus 12:1-20:

> The Lord said to Moses and Aaron in the land of Egypt, "This month shall be for you the beginning of months; it shall be the first month of the year for you. Tell the congregation of Israel that on the tenth day of this month they shall take every man a lamb according to

their father's houses, a lamb for a household; and if the household is too small for a lamb, then a man and his neighbor next to his house shall take according to the number of persons; according to what each can eat you shall make your count for the lamb. Your lamb shall be without blemish, a male a year old; you shall take it from the sheep or from the goats; and you shall keep it until the fourteenth day of this month, when the whole assembly of the congregation of Israel shall kill their lambs in the evening. Then they shall take some of the blood, and put it in the two doorposts and the lintel of the houses in which they eat them. They shall eat the flesh that night, roasted; with unleavened bread and bitter herbs they shall eat it. Do not eat any of it raw or boiled with water, but roasted, its head with its legs and its inner parts. And you shall let none of it remain until the morning, anything that remains until the morning you shall burn. In this manner you shall eat it: your loins girded, your sandals on your feet, and your staff in your hand; and you shall eat it in haste. It is the Lord's passover. For I will pass through the land of Egypt that night, and I will smite all the first-born in the land of Egypt, both man and beast; and on all the gods of Egypt I will execute judgments: I am the Lord. The blood shall be a sign for you, upon the houses where you are; and when I see the blood, I will pass over you, and no plague shall fall upon you to destroy you, when I smite the land of Egypt.

This day shall be for you a memorial day, and you shall keep it as a feast to the Lord; throughout your generations you shall observe it as an ordinance for ever. Seven days you shall eat unleavened bread; on the first day you shall put away leaven out of your houses, for if any one eats what is leavened, from the first day until the seventh day, that person shall be cut off from Israel. On the first day you shall hold a holy assembly, and on the seventh day a holy assembly; no work shall be done on those days; but what every one must eat, that only may be prepared by you. And you shall observe the feast of unleavened bread, for on this very day I brought your hosts out of the land of Egypt: therefore you shall observe this day, throughout your generations, as an ordinance for ever. In the first month, on the fourteenth day of the month at evening, you shall eat unleavened bread, and so until the twenty-first day of the month at evening. For seven days no leaven shall be found in your houses; for if any one eats what is leavened, that person shall be cut off from the congregation of Israel, whether he is a sojourner or a native of the land. You shall eat nothing leavened; in all your dwellings you shall eat unleavened bread.''

Passover, Pentecost and Tabernacles were the three major Jewish Holy Days and were celebrated with careful deliberation. The object was to remind all persons of how God had been faithful to his people in the past and to encourage them to continue to walk in the ways of God all the days of their lives. They were occasions of joyful worship, happy fellowship and feasting. Somehow we have lost sight of this idea in our day. We celebrate our holidays with gusto, but usually lose sight of the spiritual significance. What I want to suggest is that Christian families begin to make a conscious effort to recover the holy side of holidays and establish your own family traditions around these days.

For example, on Valentine's Day, for many years now around the supper table, we have had a discussion of the true meaning of love. We have a little valentines tree that we set up on the table, and most meaningful of all, each year we write poems or letters to each child telling them how and why we love them. After dinner, we read these poems aloud and sometimes go back and read the poems we have written in years past (talk about affirming your children). They love it and so do we.

On Easter, we wait until after nap time that Sunday afternoon and then we have our "Resurrection Party." We all dress up in costumes, reread the resurrection account, and then act it out, always taking movies or photographs. Then we have an Easter egg hunt and great outdoor games like an egg toss, tag or whatever.

What we are doing on these occasions is building family traditions. Your family is a unique creation of God; there will never be another like yours. We need to celebrate this incredible creation in our own particular, personalized ways. These sorts of family traditions all play their part in developing a sense of familyness, of family pride. Through them we are strengthening the bonds of family unity and building memories for the future. In a day when hitherto undreamed of mobility is possible and our jobs take us all over the face of the globe, careful thought must be given to how we are going to build strong ties of family loyalty and unity which will keep us close to one another in the years to come. All of these ideas will, in my opinion, help us do just that.

MEETING AND DISCUSSION

1. Do these suggestions about family times and family nights sound too idealistic to you? Why? Or why not?

2. Describe a recent time when your family enjoyed a particularly meaningful time of interaction or great fun. How did it come about?

FAMILY TIMES AND FAMILY NIGHTS   95

3. In response to the reading, take some time to discuss various ways individual families celebrate birthdays, special events, holidays, Holy Days, and so on.

4. In the sixth chapter of Deuteronomy, Moses relates the Lord's instructions to the people about the essence of the Law and how to communicate it with their children. Read the chapter through silently and then aloud.

   5. Look particularly at Deuteronomy verses 5–9.
      a. What strikes you as most interesting about these verses?
      b. What are some different ways families can apply these commands?
      c. What are the most difficult problems in putting these ideas into practice?

6. Verses 20–25 became a sacred part of the Jewish Passover meal celebration. Thus this is an example of how the Jews sought to celebrate a Holy Day. The Jews, as families, relived, reenacted and celebrated all the great saving acts of God in their history. Besides the obvious need to think through ways in which we, as Christian families, can do the same thing, let's think for a moment about other important events that involve us and the Lord, which we perhaps ought to be sharing with our children.
      a. Can anyone share an example of how they have tried to explain to a child how they (the parents) came into personal relationship with the Lord?
      b. Can someone (or several people) tell about ways their families have sought to remember or celebrate God's special provision for them as a *family,* or ways God has met their needs in times past? Do you have any holy places as a family? Family days that are celebrated each year in remembrance of certain blessings?

   7. What particular concerns need to be shared for prayer tonight?

CHAPTER 13

How to Talk with Your Child

Much has been made of the incredible cost in rearing children nowadays. In May of 1983, *Parade* magazine said that the average family in the United States should expect to spend $226,000 in rearing a first-born son to age 22, and $247,000 to raise a first-born daughter. In a new book, *Costs of Children* by Laurina Olson, it is estimated that families with high income will spend $323,000 on a first-born son.

As astounding as such figures are, they in no way communicate the cost of raising a child in terms of the time and energy a parent must invest. All of us know this and yet these are commitments we gladly make because we believe that children are a precious gift from the Lord.

One investment that we must all be willing and diligent to make is the care and time involved in communicating with our children. One wise pediatrician, upon being consulted by a mother of a troubled infant, wrote the following prescription: "Each day put baby outside on a blanket in the sun. Remove all clothing, except diaper. Begin with five minutes. Increase daily by five-minute periods up to one hour. *Mother must stay with child.* He knew that medication alone is not enough to produce health, that children from their infancy need the loving, available presence of their parents.

We have to make time to be alone with our children individually if we want them to sense that they are important. And it is during these times that communication can occur. A parent cannot decide when his child will open up and share from the heart. That would be nice and simplify matters a great deal but, while one child will tend to be talkative at bedtime and another during the rides home from baseball practice, we cannot program them to talk with us. We simply must take the time to be with them regularly and pray that good times of conversation will open up. A Gallup youth survey of one thousand teenagers across the nation reveals that 25 percent do not discuss their day's activities with their parents. Forty-two percent said they had not received parental words of praise during the twenty-four-hour reporting period. Half had not gotten a hug or kiss and 54 percent had not heard the words, "I love you." Seventy-nine percent said they had not been helped with homework by a parent. (*Dads Only,* March 1981) Who can say how accurate such satistics are? But such statistics consistently keep reappearing. For instance, *The Family Concern Bulletin* reported: "Of 600 teens who attended a venereal disease clinic in New York City, only 21 percent said they had received any sex information from their parents. *Homemade* magazine, May 1977, reported: "Of 200 college students surveyed—91 percent said parents had given them no instruction about dating; 43 percent no instruction whatsoever on sex; 82 percent no warning about drinking, smoking, using drugs; 83 percent no instruction at all about the use of money."

I am hesitant to discuss this as I feel that this is an area in which I often fail as a parent. But what I know to be true I will share.

Perhaps most important is the attitude with which we view our children. Do we see them as "Very Important Persons"? Many writers of our day have spoken of the rampant "epidemic of inferiority," the fact that so many young persons suffer from a low sense of personal worth. Our society worships at the triple temples of brains, brawn and beauty, and children who are not generously endowed in any of these areas are going to have a difficult time believing that they are important and have a contribution to make in life. We parents have got to let them know that *we* think they are the most important people in the whole world. "Honey," we've got to say, "you are my greatest claim to fame! Being *your* dad is the highest privilege of my life!"

If they are assured of this over and over, they will feel secure in our love and able to open up and share with us. But the reverse is also true. The American Institute of Family Relations reported a survey in which parents were asked to record how many negative, as opposed to positive, comments they made to their children. The results showed that they criticized ten times for every favorable comment. In a survey in Orlando, Florida, teachers were found to be 75 percent negative. And it was learned that it takes four positive statements from a teacher to offset the effects of one negative statement to a child. (*Dads Only,* January 1980)

There are many levels of communication, and just talking with our children does not guarantee effective communication. One can speak in generalities or cliches and reveal very little about himself:

"How was your day today?"

"Fine."

"What did you do?"

"Nothing."

"Well, how are you doing, son?"

"Okay."

I believe the parents must take the lead in sharing at a deeper level with their children if they want to get to know, really know, this young person who is their own flesh and blood. We must take the time and trouble to share from our own lives and experience, discussing some of our own feelings and questions, and the causes of our own joy or disappointment if we want them to share similarly with us.

This means that in a way a parent must talk to his child as though the child were a fellow adult. I don't mean that we should burden them with the sort of information that will produce fear or insecurity, but rather that we speak to them as *equals* whose opinions and insights we value highly.

I can vividly remember my mother sharing things in *confidence* with me that I doubted any other child in town knew about.

"Son, this is something I don't want you to talk about with your friends, but I think it will help you to understand that. . . ."

"Honey, you are mature enough to understand that. . . . Many of your friends, however, *wouldn't* be mature enough to see this. . . ."

Often a child will sense that something is wrong, someone has a problem, or there is trouble in the air. It will cause that child to think of himself as important, mature and confidante if his parent occasionally takes him aside and explains the whole truth to him. The child will feel important.

Suppose Uncle Bill is an alcoholic. He comes to visit and periodically becomes tipsy or worse. Do you simply pretend nothing is wrong and not discuss it with the child? When the child asks what is the matter with Uncle Bill, do you make up an excuse? I think not. Far better to tell your child the truth in a way in which he can understand and get the child to join you in praying for Uncle Bill. Conversations like this convey to the child that we *trust* them, that we have confidence in them to understand and share in something which is important to all of us. Knowing we consider them trustworthy will help them to become, in fact, worthy of our trust.

Certainly we must always seek to maintain the proper balance between "telling the whole truth" and "keeping" something from our child because of the fear or insecurity which might result. My observation is, however, that often we err on the side of keeping secrets from our children. They need to know that we consider them important enough to be let in on some of these secrets. One educational psychologist interviewed more than 250 children between the ages of four and seventeen. Her findings indicate that:

> Almost all wish their families talked more. Among the older children, talking with parents is considered the best way to gain insight on issues that have no clear right or wrong answer.
>
> The most unanimously negative feeling about non-communication comes from not being told about crucial matters, especially such family matters as death or divorce. And any discussion that degenerates into anger or judgment is not popular.
>
> There are eight main topics that they wish their parents would talk about more, and that are of major concern to them.
> 1. Family matters.
> 2. Controversial issues. Sex, drugs, homosexuality—all issues we fail to discuss with children because they make us uncomfortable. However, the children interviewed overwhelmingly want to know about these things. Related to the controversial topics are "values" issues. Why are certain things right and others wrong?
> 3. Emotional issues. In every group of children who participated, someone brought up the fact that he wishes his parents would tell him they love him.
> 4. The Big Whys
> 5. The Future
> 6. Personal interests. Many of the children interviewed say they wish their parents would show concern about what they do and like.
> 7. Parents themselves. Stories about the parent when young, particularly those stories that emphasize the parent's emotional side or human failings, apparently have great appeal (Tory Haydon "Conversation Kids Crave" in *Families Magazine,* June 1982 pp. 66-72).

Why not seek their advice, their insights on certain things? Obviously, you don't go to your child to get his sage thoughts on your next stock market venture, but suppose you are having a problem with a neighbor, suppose the neighbor is angry about some neighborly misunderstanding. Why *not* discuss is with your child? Sooner or later they are going to have to learn about such things. Occasionally it is good to share them with our children, and to ask them to pray for you and with you to have wisdom to know how to respond.

Why *not* talk to your child about your investments? Or your concerns about buying a new car? Not that the child should have to hear the technical details, but it seems to me that children will not be prepared to make adult decisions if we adults never discuss *our* adult concerns with them. Four out of ten teenagers say their views are either ignored or bypassed. They say their parents are often reluctant to acknowledge their competence, good judgment or good intentions. (*Families Magazine,* March 1982.)

All of this is to say that if we cultivate the habit of talking, in depth, about our own selves, they will be likely to feel freer to talk about themselves. If my Chris knows that I get uptight and have to pray before I take a trip on an airplane, he will feel freer to say that he's frightened by the neighbor's dog. If my 11-year-old daughter knows that I'm self-conscious about something, she'll realize I can understand her own self-consciousness. The beloved Fred Rogers of "Mr. Rogers' Neighborhood" has said: "Raising kids today is quite a demanding task, but parents should not feel they have to flock to psychological and sociological "experts" who seem to have all the answers. The experts in many ways have done a disservice . . . parents have been afraid to be who they really are with their kids and that is the most important thing." (*Dads Only,* May 1978)

A parent shouldn't speak to his child as though the child were an adult also, but as though the child is a confidante, a close and valued friend, one with whom we *want* to share our hearts. This will improve their "I sight" immeasurably. The following is a good creed for how we ought to relate to our children.

Children Learn What They Live

If a child lives with criticism, he learns to condemn.
If a child lives with hostility, he learns to fight.
If a child lives with ridicule, he learns to be shy.
If a child lives with shame, he learns to feel guilty.
If a child lives with tolerance, he learns to be patient.
If a child lives with encouragement, he learns confidence.
If a child lives with praise, he learns to appreciate.
If a child lives with fairness, he learns justice.
If a child lives with security, he learns to have faith.
If a child lives with approval, he learns to like himself.
If a child lives with acceptance and friendship,
He learns to find love in the world.

Dorothy Law Nolte

We don't kid ourselves that this is easy. One specialist in the field of human behavior has said that "it probably takes more endurance, more patience, more healthy emotion, to rear a happy human being than it does to be an atomic physicist or a politician or a psychiatrist."

DON'T BE SURPRISED

I was struck by the following account of a mother in Bethesda, Maryland, particularly because we too have a balcony in our church, and I could imagine my own kids having similar fantasies.

> After church last Sunday, Peter confided to me that he sometimes had this terrible fear that he might jump off the balcony during the church service to land in the lap of some startled lady below.
>
> I know exactly what he's talking about. When I was young, sitting stone-still beside my mother in church, resisting the awful urge to scratch or kick my legs or lick all the offertory envelopes in the rack on the pew in front, I sometimes had the terrible thought that I might irresistibly rise from my seat, give a blood-curdling yell, and go cartwheeling down the aisle to the altar.
>
> It was not just a terrible thought—it was a recurring nightmare that kept me glued to my seat, and that made me grip the edges of the pew in a deathlock and forced me to always take an inside seat so that, should the wolfman in me get the upper hand, my mother could grab me before I reached the aisle.
>
> And still that fantasy absorbed me. I would imagine the startled pause of the minister as I gave my war whoop. I would imagine the stares of the women as I rose from my seat and bolted for the aisle. I would imagine the horror on the faces of the men as I cartwheeled down to the altar. And finally, I could imagine the ushers rushing forward and escorting me out the side door while my embarrassed family sat paralyzed in the pew.
>
> I confided it all to my mother once, and it helped immeasurably. She said that it was simply nature's way of working off a small girl's tension during a long sermon, and that fantasizing it helped insure that it would never really come about. But if it should, she said, God would understand.
>
> Somehow the fear dissipated. Somehow the thought of yelling and cartwheeling down the aisle, only to be met with calm understanding faces once I got there, took the zest out of the whole idea. And that's why I told Peter that if he ever jumped off the balcony and landed in a lady's lap, we would understand.
>
> He stared at me a full half-minute before he turned on his heels and went back outside.

"It was a lousy idea," he muttered. But he's sure to think up a replacement. (Copyright *Family Life Today* magazine, Pasadena, California. Reprinted by permission.)

Learning to listen and at least appear to understand such wild revelations from our children is one of the qualities our children will appreciate from us.

QUESTIONS AND ANSWERS

Learning how to ask good questions of our children is a vital task, for all too often a child does not simply volunteer information. Often after asking, "How was your day?" and "How is school?" we run out of questions and yet feel we really still haven't penetrated beneath the skin of superficiality. We must pray for creativity and imagination in this matter and then push on. I find it helpful to raise questions in the area of relationships and schedules. For example:

RELATIONSHIPS:

"Who's your favorite teacher these days? Tell me some of the reasons why?"

"What's Jill doing these days? Why is she so involved in swimming? How does she feel about it? Does that appeal to you? Why? Why not?"

"I was noticing that new boy Bill at the ballgame the other night. How is he getting along in your class? How are people responding to him? What's he like? Have you gotten to know him? What do you think of him? Could he become one of your close friends?"

SCHEDULES:

"Today I spent all morning in a meeting with the Board of Directors. It went really well. What were you doing at 11:00 this morning? I was thinking of you about then. . . . Who else was there with you? How did it go? Do you feel you did well? Do you think the others knew you were lonely? I remember once when I. . . . Did you ever try handling it that way? How do you think it would work?"

"Mom told me you won your soccer match today. Tell me about it—from the first quarter to the last. Who played the best? Did the coach have anything to say to you? How did you feel when he said that? I know what you mean, I think. Are you saying that. . . .? What would happen if you. . . .?"

All of this implies that the parent is listening with an active ear, trying to get inside the thoughts and feelings of his child and truly understand. Again, this produces a sense of importance and self-worth in the child. It is so easy to assume that we know what our children are doing and thinking and to forget that they are changing and growing all the time. We think that we understand our child's feelings. We make decisions which will affect our children assuming we know what will please or upset them, but are we really all that clearly tuned in?

A University of Arizona psychologist questioned some 367 fourth, fifth and sixth graders in an attempt to ascertain what were some of the troublesome thoughts and experiences on their minds. Here are the youngsters' ratings (with "14" the most stressful):

13.8	Losing a parent
13.7	Going blind
13.6	Being held back in school
13.5	Wetting your pants in school
13.4	Hearing parents quarrel
13.3	Being caught stealing
13.1	Being suspected of lying
12.5	Receiving a bad report card
11.5	Being sent to the principal's office
11.0	Having an operation
11.0	Getting lost
10.6	Being made fun of in class
9.2	Moving to a new school
8.2	Having a scary dream
7.5	Not getting 100 on a test
6.6	Being picked last for a team
6.3	Losing in a game
5.5	Going to the dentist
5.1	Giving a report in class
2.5	Acquiring a baby sibling

(Geraldine Carro, "What Worries Kids Most" in *Ladies Home Journal;* June 1980, p. 126)

Most adults and even many professionals who deal with children often misread their child's feelings. Parents, for example, would often think that the arrival of a new baby would produce a great deal of stress, while hearing parents quarrel would be fairly routine and unstressful. Not so, according to this particular study.

The point is what we should listen *very* carefully to our children in an effort to understand what they are feeling and experiencing. By the time they are in the fourth or fifth grade, they are already able to be included in much of the family decision making which will affect them.

Such listening involves concentration and restraint. I must keep asking myself, "What are they saying?" "What does this emotion tell me?" "Are they afraid? angry? bored?" I must refrain from criticizing them or interrupting if I am really to hear and understand.

I doubt very seriously that we parents in this incredibly full, fast-paced century can listen to our children in this way unless we plan ahead to have time with our children. For years now I have made appointments with my children in my pocket calendar and taken them as seriously as the counseling appointments and meetings that fill up on the days recorded there.

I seem to have some times when the weeks are so full that it is all I can do to be civil to my family, let alone make time to be with them individually, but I keep trying and so, I believe, we must all. This is not quite so hard for a parent who is at home during the day, but it is easy even for the housewife, too, to become so occupied with the daily chores and regular interruptions that she does not take time to be alone with the children individually. Even after the twins entered a preschool nursery class three days a week, Susan would still keep one of them at home with her one school morning every other week just to have that little one close to her with no other siblings around.

When I say make appointments with our children, I simply mean, week by week, to think ahead and mark off a time to be with your child for some special purpose that will appeal to him. It may be to plan to go fly a kite on Sunday afternoon, or to go out to breakfast at the diner Friday before school, or to go and spend an hour at the library after supper on Tuesday night. Chances are that if we don't plan it ahead of time, and commit to it, some unexpected something will come up and the outing will never materalize.

In these outings, over the years, I believe that the relationships which are forged will become secure and mutually enlightening. Talking will become easier. Although there will be periods when your child will not want to talk at all, that is all right. The important thing is that he will know you are his friend and that he is crucially important to you.

MEETING AND DISCUSSION

1. Take fifteen minutes to discuss what stands out as most helpful to you in the reading for this week.

2. Now, let's take some time for personal assessment. Individually rate your communication with your child or one of your children using the following:

Child's Name: _____

	all the time	most of the time	little of the time
a. I know how this child is spending his time	_____	_____	_____
b. I know the people this child is with	_____	_____	_____
c. This child talks to me about his activities	_____	_____	_____
d. . . . about his friends	_____	_____	_____
e. . . . about his feelings	_____	_____	_____
f. . . . about his convictions	_____	_____	_____
g. I feel very close to this child	_____	_____	_____

h. During the last week, the two of us have had a good visit alone:

_____ each day   _____ nearly everyday

_____ only once or twice   _____ not at all

i. My child knows what I'm doing, how I spend my time:

_____ most of the time

_____ part of the time

_____ rarely

j. I pray with this child _____ daily, _____ regularly, _____ rarely.

k. In our communication, I am concerned about *this child's:*

_____ willingness to open up

_____ sense of his own importance

_____ sense of closeness to his own parents.

_____ other

l. I am concerned about *my*

_____ ability to ask good questions

_____ ability to really listen

_____ lack of time with this child

_____ inability to understand _____

_____ about this child.

other _____

3. When you have completed this, then discuss your answers with your mate. Single parents pair up with each other or with a couple. Ask any clarifying questions that will help you to understand better what your mate is saying.

4. Come back together and ask if there are any concerns that have been shared which anyone would like to raise for discussion or advice among the whole group.

5. How has this study prompted you to want to work on your communication with your child? Let each person share one positive step they feel God would have them take. How? When?

6. Close with prayer, each person praying for the one with whom he has been talking tonight.

CHAPTER 14

The Question of Discipline

A few years back, the Swedish Parliament, by an overwhelming vote, passed a law prohibiting parents from striking their children or treating them in a humiliating way. Slapping, spanking and whacking are all now forbidden. "Humiliating treatment" apparently includes such activities as sending children to bed without supper. This legislation was supposed to raise public consciousness on *better* ways to discipline children, and the law does not prescribe punishment for parents who break it. The one concession made to parents was they still retain the right to show anger!

Recently, an older gentleman whom I greatly respect was ruminating on child raising and discipline, and said to me, "You know, as I reflect upon it, I don't believe I ever gained a thing by physically disciplining my children. . . . I rather wish I'd never punished them in that way."

I have a vivid memory from childhood of being "switched" on the legs by my mother with a stiff little branch from the tree that grew just outside our kitchen door. I never remember being spanked in anger or without an explanation, and I don't recall ever feeling that the parent doing the punishing did not love me. It was always clearly communicated to me that this was to teach me a lesson for my own welfare, and I believed it. I still do.

What *is* the right way to exert discipline with our children? *Is* there a right way? There seems to be a good deal in the Bible about not "sparing the rod" in order not to spoil the child. What is the role of the rod? When should it be used? When not?

I see two main reasons for disciplining children. One reason discipline is important is that it is necessary in order to teach a child to make wise choices and to live in harmony with others, to help our children develop self-discipline and personal wisdom.

The other reason for discipline is to enable a child to learn to submit to the authority of his parents so that as he grows the child will be obedient to God in his Christian life. If a child is disobedient to his parents then he will certainly not obey God whom he cannot see and whose expectations are the very highest.

The writer of Hebrews said that God "disciplines us for our good that we may share his holiness" (Hebrews 12:10). So also a parent must discipline his child, but as he does he must be asking himself, "How can I best help my child learn from his situation?" Suppose your child wilfully disobeys a family rule. Just to punish the child doesn't necessarily teach him the reason why his action was wrong. Ongoing discipline must be educational or the child will profit very little. We need always to keep this in mind as occasions arise in which it is necessary to exert discipline.

Several years ago Dennis Guernsey wrote a thought-provoking article entitled, "What Kind of a Parent Are You?" (*Family Life Today* magazine, January, 1975; p. 5, 6 and 29) He reported that researches into family life found that the two most powerful factors influencing children were parental control and parental support. *Control* was defined as the ability of a parent to manage a child's behavior; and *support* as the ability to make the child feel loved. To get these two qualities together is crucially important.

Because we vary in our abilities to combine these qualities, Guernsey explains that there are generally four kinds of parents, described in the following chart:

Parents who were *high* in support but *low* in control were called "permissive."

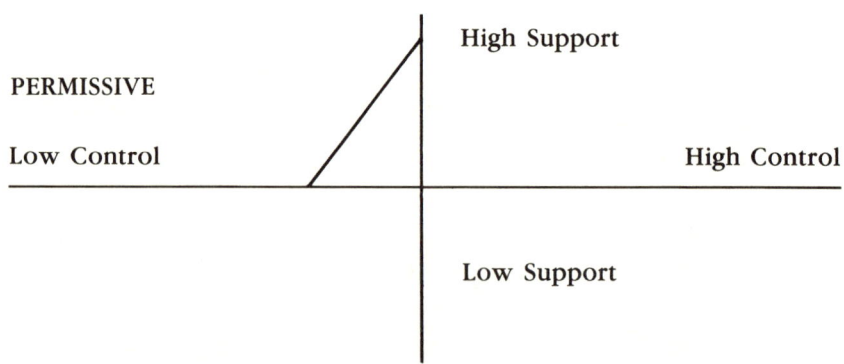

THE QUESTION OF DISCIPLINE   109

Parents who were *low* in support and *low* in control
were termed "neglectful."

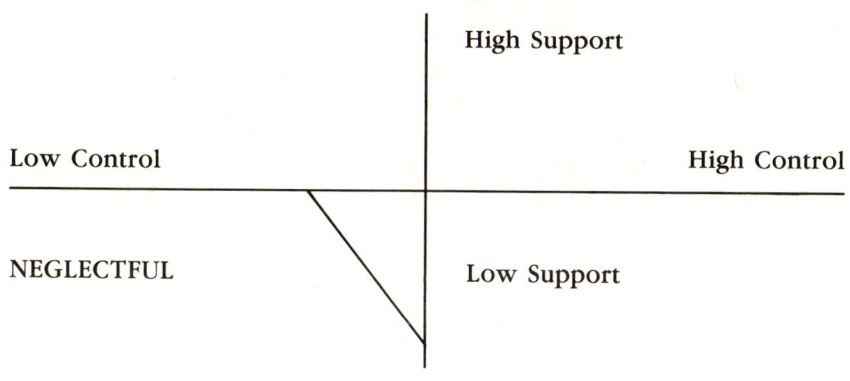

Parents *high* in control but *low* in support
were called "authoritarian."

Parents *high* in support and *high* in control
were called "authoritative."

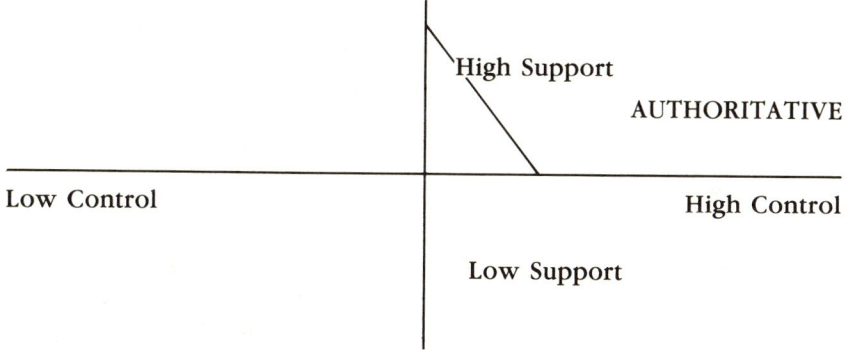

(*Family Life Today* magazine, January 1978. Charts used by permission.)

In answer to the question, "What sorts of kids are *produced* by these types of parents, some interesting conclusions followed. I will only relate them briefly.

In the area of self-worth the *authoritative* parents (high support, high control) scored highest—#1, with convincing evidence that they raised children with the most secure sense of self-respect. The *permissive* parents (low control, high support) scored #2; *authoritarian* (high control and low support) were #3; while *neglectful* (low control, low support) had the lowest rating, #4.

In raising children who are able to conform to the authority of others, the *authoritative* parents again scored highest—#1. *Permissive,* #2; while the *neglectful* parents was #3 in this area and the *authoritarian* parent rated lowest, #4.

When it came to children who tended to accept their parents' faith, the *authoritative* parent again showed the greatest positive influence with the score of #1.

Later in the article, Guernsey says:

As the men gave this report on their findings, all of a sudden it hit me: 'Whom the Lord loves, he chastens.' He is always supportive, loving me with an everlasting love. Because of His love, He has established the controls I need for an abundant, everlasting life. God disciplines me when I don't obey and stray from the way He's established. What a model for parenting!

If you want to grow good children who have opportunities for a long and satisfying life you need to give them support and control. The child whose parents lovingly establish limits and controls for him to obey has the greatest opportunity to realize God's promise in Ephesians 6:3 of a "long life, full of blessing" (originally published in *Family Life Today* magazine, January 1975).

God does not put love in opposition to discipline; he combines the two. Discipline grows out of love. Without love, discipline is hard and cruel, but love without discipline is just sentimentality. When a parent has maintained a strong, loving relationship with his child, then the situations which demand corrective discipline will actually bring the parent and child closer together.

My four-year-old Susie has a way of showing me this that I find completely overwhelming. Often, when she has misbehaved and is in tears and I am in the process of disciplining her, she reaches out to me with both arms as if saying, "Now Daddy, I need you to hug me." I am hoping that even at four she knows my discipline does spring from love.

The writer to the Hebrews said something very interesting. "We had earthly fathers to discipline us and we respected them" (12:9). Evidently he had respect for his earthly father because he knew, in being disciplined, that his father cared for him. If our children can see this, then they will grow to one day appreciate the discipline we have given them just as this writer did.

The means by which we discipline our children surely must change as they become older. When a child is very young, it seems to me that there are times when restrained physical spanking is the most effective way to communicate that an action is unacceptable. But as time passes, other means of discipline become more appropriate. Once or twice I have been so completely defeated in my attempts to bring to an end one of my children's violent temper tantrums, that I have bodily taken them into the bathroom, turned on the cold water, and placed them under it! In the two times I can remember doing this, I do recollect that on one occasion, the remedy was quite effective and on the other, totally ineffective! (Shutting them up in their room usually works best.)

Whatever methods of discipline we use, I am certain that it is crucially important to remember three things: First, that we let our children know what we expect, what is acceptable behavior.

Second, we must be consistent. All too often the severity of the punishment depends on the physical or emotional state of the parent. If you chasten your son on Tuesday for interrupting you on the telephone, then when your daughter does the same thing on Friday, she should get comparable discipline. If a rule is worth having, it is worth enforcing.

Third, we must always seek to reaffirm our love for the child in the midst of the discipline. Perhaps we should think of this whole process in the same way we think of training a child to ride horseback or play baseball. We have plenty of patience in teaching a new skill because we accept and even expect mistakes. Perhaps we should see our children's misbehavior in the light of a learning experience more than we do. The tricky thing here, however, is that we are talking about a way of living, which is more than just a skill. A Christian must live in obedience to God and in a real sense, every Christian's will (self-centeredness) must be "broken" if we are going to submit to the Lordship of Christ in our lives.

We do not want to "beat" our children into obedience to us any more than God wants our cowering resignation to His "pathway." God wants us to rejoice in the wisdom of His commandments and gladly walk in His way. So too, we want our children to make responsible decisions and live a happy life in keeping with the principles and virtues which we teach them. But realistically, sometimes, children do not "see the light" or the wisdom of our teaching until they are older. In the meantime, appropriate behavior must be enforced by parents through firm discipline.

THE CONSEQUENCES OF DISOBEDIENCE

As children get older and assume responsibility for their own actions, it becomes more and more important that they learn to make their own decisions in the best way regardless of whether a parent is present.

Rudolf Dreikurst and Loren Grey have pursued this line of thinking in *A Parents' Guide to Child Discipline* (New York, Hawthorn Books, 1970). Some of their students have developed a method of parent training called "Systematic Training for Effective Parenting" which has been used in study groups around the country. One of the ideas they develop quite effectively is this concept of the "natural and logical consequences" of misbehavior. The idea is that we ought to work very hard at helping our children early on to see the *consequences* of their misbehavior: eat no supper and you'll go hungry; wear no mittens in the snow and your hands will soon become very cold. The reality of the consequences will, they say, teach the child the proper behavior, and will also encourage children to make their own responsible decisions.

I'm not so sure that this is a "modern thing" (I can still hear the crusty old farmer saying of the child playing too near the horse's hindquarters, "Let him alone, he'll learn"), nor am I sure that it is always the best one, for, as we have said, a Christian must learn obedience as *well* as responsibility. We must learn to *obey* God even if we aren't altogether certain that the commandment is right; the clay doesn't question the potter. Still, this matter of a child's learning through consequences does have much merit in developing responsible decision making.

I find the following concepts intriguing. (Summarized from the *Parents Handbook* of the Systematic Training for Effective Parenting Program Don Dinkmeyer and Gary McKay. American Guidance Service, Inc., Circle Pines, MN, 1976.)

1. Rewards and punishments deny children the opportunity to make their own decisions, to be responsible for their own behavior.

2. Realizing natural and logical consequences of misbehavior can help children to be responsible for their own behavior.

3. *Natural consequences* are those which permit children to learn from the natural order of the physical world. For example, that not sleeping is followed by tiredness.

4. *Logical consequences* are those which enable children to learn from

the reality of the social order. For example, children who do not get to ball practice on time may be benched and unable to play.

5. For consequences to be effective in helping children become responsible, the children involved must see them as logical. Using natural and logical consequences can motivate children to make responsible decisions.

6. Parents should be both firm and kind. Firmness refers to your followthrough behavior; kindness denotes the manner in which you present the choice.

7. When you do things for children that they can do themselves, you are robbing them of self-respect and responsibility.

Those who teach this system of child-rearing see some differences between punishment and logical consequences as a means of training children. They see the concept of punishment as a negative one because it stresses the power of personal authority; it sometimes communicates to the child that he or she is bad. Further, it is felt that punishment is a poor concept since it demands obedience rather than permits choice. Proponents of the "logical consequences" school would say parents ought always to provide choices and accept the child's own decision, following through with the consequences and in a friendly tone of voice assuring the children that they may try again later.

Now while we certainly appreciate what this system is seeking to achieve, we must see this system from the following perspective. Parents are, by God's design, the authorities in the home. No Christian is his own ultimate authority however, as Christ must be king in our lives. If we love him, we will keep his commandments. Obedience is a crucial lesson to learn if we are going to follow in Christ's way. The social order is not our barometer of right and wrong. It is very important, but obedience to Christ is the ultimate aim.

Punishment need not tell a child that he/she is bad. In fact, it can indeed stress that he/she is good and important. If parents are unwilling to enforce their moral judgments they rob their children of a clear understanding of right and wrong.

The value of this "consequence" approach is, however, that it does wisely stress the importance of our children learning to think for themselves. The sooner we are able to help them do this, the better. But to allow them to make all their own choices and simply experience the "discipline" of logical and natural consequences, may be teaching them that there is no God and no ultimate standard of right and wrong behavior by which we will be judged.

A couple of typical child-raising problems and possible ways of handling them will serve to help us understand how this concept (logical consequence) of childraising works:

The Problem: The child is late for meals.

Typical Reactions:
> Call several times, lecture, feed them after everyone else has finished, or send them to bed without supper.

Natural and Logical Consequences:
> Allow children to be responsible for getting themselves to meals. Tell them that meals will be served at specific times. Say that you will call them once and that it's up to them to decide whether or not to come. If they are going to be away from home, inform them what time the meal will be served and let them be responsible for checking the time. If the meal is still being served when the children arrive, they may eat. (The consequence would be eating cold food.) If they miss the meal, they should go without food until the next meal, so that they will experience the natural consequences of hunger. The choice of whether or not to come to a meal on time—or to come at all—remains theirs.

Explanation:
> Continuing to call children several times, or searching for them when they don't show up, is giving them undue service. Lecturing or arbitrarily sending them to bed undermines the parent-child relationship. Heating their food or serving them after the rest of the family has finished also provides undue service and fails to teach them to be responsible for their own behavior.

Another Problem: Coming to the table dirty.

Typical Reactions:
> Lecture, send away from table to wash.

Natural and Logical Consequences:
> Tell children that if they wish to come to the table, they will need to be clean. If they arrive dirty, simply remove their plates and say, "I see you are not ready to eat." Say no more. Do not return the plates until the children are clean. If they are not clean by the conclusion of the meal, assume they have decided to skip the meal and tell them they may try again at the next meal. Prevent snacking before the next meal.

Explanation:
> Coming to the table clean is the children's responsibility. You act with firmness by calmly removing their plates and allowing them to decide whether they intend to eat.

MEETING AND DISCUSSION

Why not begin the discussion by praying that the Lord would instruct you. Then use the following questions as a guide for discussion. Read Ephesians 6:4:

> And now, a word to you parents. Don't keep on scolding and nagging your children, making them angry and resentful. Rather, bring them up with the loving discipline the Lord himself approves, with suggestions and godly advice.

1. What are the two different approaches to child raising that Paul mentions?

2. What is "loving discipline"?

3. What is love without discipline likely to produce?

4. What is discipline without love likely to produce?

5. What do you think is the ultimate *purpose* of child discipline? Please read the following quotes from Proverbs and jot down in the margin any questions they raise in your mind.

> Young man, obey your father and your mother. Take to heart all their advice; keep in mind everything they tell you. Every day and all night long their counsel will lead you and save you from harm; when you wake up in the morning, let their instructions guide you into the new day. For their advice is a beam of light directed into the dark corners of your mind to warn you of danger and to give you a good life (Proverbs 6:20–24).
>
> If you refuse to discipline your son, it proves you don't love him; for if you love him you will be prompt to punish him (Proverbs 13:24).
>
> Discipline your son in his early years while there is hope. If you don't you will ruin his life. A short-tempered man must bear his own penalty; you can't do much to help him. If you try once you must try a dozen times! (Proverbs 19:18–19).
>
> A youngster's heart is filled with rebellion, but punishment will drive it out of him (Proverbs 22:15).

Don't fail to correct your children; discipline won't hurt them! They won't die if you use a stick on them! Punishment will keep them out of hell (Proverbs 23:13–14).

6. When do you begin (at what age) to punish children?

7. When does physical punishment stop and other kinds of punishment replace it? (At what age?)

8. I suggest that you divide into smaller groups and discuss any particular problems with any of your children in the areas of:

   temper
   deceit
   honesty
   bad language
   disobedience

9. In what ways are you dealing (or not dealing) with it?

10. What advice would you like from the group?

CHAPTER 15

A Word to Husbands and Fathers

Several years after we were married, my wife said something which surprised me very much. Before I tell you what it was, allow me to give you a little background.

Earlier in this book, I shared the story of how hard it was for me to accept the extraordinary capabilities of my wife without being defensive. In some ways, it seems she was much better at things related to my chosen profession than I. One of the major reasons I found this difficult was due to a fundamental *misconception* of mine about the role of the husband.

The Bible speaks clearly and repeatedly about the husband/father as "head" of the house. I used to assume this meant that I should be wiser and more knowledgeable than my wife, and that I should basically make the major decisions about our family life. The trouble was that this didn't seem to fit with the facts in our home, so gradually I subconsciously "threw out" that idea of "headship."

Then, one day, Susan said, out of the blue, "Honey, I'm so glad that I can look to you as the head of our home."

I had no earthly idea what she was talking about. Hadn't that idea gone out with the E.R.A. and women's rights? I quickly requested an amplification for my edification, and her explanation not only surprised me but opened my eyes to a whole new understanding.

"I can depend on you always to keep our family going on the right track. You not only set an example for me of consistency in your Christian walk, but you are like a rudder on a ship. I know that as long as you are with us, we'll always go in the right direction. I have tremendous respect for your commitment to be God's man, no matter what. That's how you are the head of our home."

This was several years ago, but the conversation remains in my mind. It was, of course, a wonderful encouragement to me, but also quite helpful in my understanding of "headship."

Without reviewing all the many relevant passages, we recall that at various points in Scripture, the father is exhorted, not only to be the provider and protector of the family, but also to be the teacher, the disciplinarian, the encourager of his children, and the one responsible for the religious instruction of his children. In this day of the working wife, we are placing much stress on *equality* of husband and wife, and on working out each individual couple's own sort of system in relationship to household and parental duties. Because of this, the biblical emphasis on the *man's* responsibility in all these things seems somehow out of tune. Some have chosen to discard some of these notions as being rooted more in the patriarchal customs of the biblical days rather than rooted necessarily in the mind of God for all time.

But, my wife's words to me long ago helped me to get all this a little more clearly into focus in my own mind. Headship as a father or husband does not imply superiority in any way, nor does it mean every husband and every wife are to divide up family duties in just the same way. They are, I believe, to share them in the way that fits best with their schedules. Headship does not mean bossiness. It does, I believe, imply that the father/husband has a certain responsibility to God for the care and well-being of his family, that ultimately he is accountable to God for his family. But, the emphasis is not so much on a certain role which he is to fulfill as it is on his relationship to his wife and family. This comes out quite clearly in two New Testament passages.

First: "The husband is the head of the wife as Christ is the head of the Church" (Ephesians 5:23). What does this mean?

There are some ways in which this analogy *cannot* be true and therefore *cannot* be what St. Paul meant. Christ had absolute and unlimited authority (see Colossians 1:15–17). No husband has that. Christ had full and unbroken fellowship with the Father and, therefore, always saw things from God's perspective. We dads don't. Christ was perfect in actions and in attitudes. None of us are.

Therefore, the headship of a husband/father does not mean we always make all the decisions as a sort of bureaucratic dictator. Not only are we often wrong, furthermore, our children will never become responsible if we try to make all their decisions for them.

One of my friends is in this situation now; she warns me that any of these answers is a conversation killer. Of course we agree that we'd rather be out of a conversation with anyone who considered it killed at that point.

The tenor of the women's movement has changed a great deal, but all of us are affected by the women's liberation movement in ways we are just vaguely aware of, even conservative, Christian, small-town women and their conservative, loving husbands as well!

Ibsen summed up the underlying question in a prophetic statement by Helmer in *A Doll's House,* when he says: "Before everything else you are a wife and a mother." Nora replies, "I don't believe that any longer. I believe that before everything else I am a human being just as much as you are. At any rate I shall try to become one."

Women and mothers are greatly concerned, as I see it, with experiencing in life the full breadth of what it means to develop their human or, for Christians, God-given potentials. This is a worthwhile concern for anyone, male or female, but it seems to be leading many Christian women and mothers into some brackish waters.

The most obvious current example is the myth of the "successful woman" or the "super mom." Every time you pick up certain magazines, here is another article enthusiastically extolling these "successful women." The themes are by now pretty familiar. A woman breaks into a traditionally "male" profession, works very hard, earns a high salary, and, if married, is able to hire full-time housekeeping help so she can have "quality time" with her children. Fallows, commenting on this phenomena, writes:

> When I encounter Successful Women like these in magazine articles, their lives sound seamless and perfect. They insist that if it ever came to a hard choice, the family and children would come first— but it never seems to come to a hard choice. There is no room for a sick mother requiring care, or for a husband who isn't supportive and helpful, or for serious and unexpected problems with the children. These women haven't had to give up anything they really wanted.
>
> But even in the most toast-of-the-town female success stories, there's something left out. We photograph these women only from their best angles—and we drop out the choices they make and the costs they pay.
>
> I'm glad to be a part of a generation of women who are free to make choices about careers and families. However, as far as I can tell, the seamless web of family-and-prestigious-career just doesn't work. At some point, you have to sit down and decide

CHAPTER 16

A Word to Mothers

A man rarely gives much thought to all the various challenges and difficulties of motherhood until his wife gets sick or goes home to visit "Mother" for a few days, leaving him with the kids (or until he has to write down his thoughts on motherhood). As I have reflected, from time to time, upon motherhood, I am struck time and time again by the current turmoil in our culture surrounding the whole concept of motherhood. It's not just that *being* a mother to children is tough, but nowadays the whole social concept of femininity and motherhood is undergoing universal transition.

Floating and flailing along in the backwaters left by the more militant feminists of our day are millions of women who are restless in their search for a woman's identity. "Just being a mother" is a concept which has had remarkably bad press for the last fifteen years and most young mothers nowadays struggle with how to answer the question of "What do you do?"

In a 1980 article in *The Washington Monthly,* Deborah Fallows writes:

> When people ask me what I do, my answer is safe and fashionable: I tell them my job title (I am an assistant dean at Georgetown University) and add that my son keeps me busy in my time after work.
>
> But I know how the world works, and I'm embarrassed that I already worry about what I'll answer next year, when the truth is that I'll be at home raising two children and otherwise unemployed. What do I say then? 'I'm a linguist but I'm taking time off to raise the children now' or 'I don't work anymore because we have two children?'

In New York magazine, we heard a director of a fertility clinic who handles requests for artificial insemination even boasting about their clients' superior taste: "Our single recipients are bright, talented superwomen who refuse to settle for just any man in order to get married and have a baby."

It appears that the women's need to have a child came first, before their understanding of a child's need to have a father.

It is true that life is full of accidents, unplanned pregnancies, divorce, and desertion. But there is surely a difference between a divorced father and no father.

I understand the motives of women, disillusioned or discouraged at the prospects for shared parenthood, who decide to give up hoping and go "it" alone. But these new unwed mothers have done more than abandon the traditional.

They have embraced the notion that fathers are the dispensable, disposable parents, handy but not vital. Perhaps that is true for some mothers. Perhaps it has been true for some fathers. But it's not true for the children.

Children don't give up hoping so easily. They cannot rationalize their needs so articulately. The babies and toddlers photographed with mothers in these articles about their "elective parent" have yet to be interviewed. But they are likely to grow up with a built-in longing in their lives—likely to grow up missing something, missing the unnamed, unknown someone their friends call father.

What does it mean to deliberately bring a generation of fatherless children into the world? Before we accept this so easily as just another option, we should ask the accident victims. Ask them about their Father's Day.

("The New Fatherless" in *The Washington Post,* June 14, 1983).

Perhaps the most tragic statement of the decline or, even perhaps, the loss of fatherhood in Western culture is the fact that it is not even necessary now for a woman to obtain the consent of her child's father before having it aborted, whether she is married or not.

I doubt if ever in history there has been a period in which Christian husbands and fathers faced greater challenges. The need for men to commit themselves to Christian fathering and Christian "husbanding" is crucial. Men, have the courage to assume your responsibilities under God in your home. Examine your schedules, listen to your wives, listen to your children. Unless you aggressively and creatively give your best to your family, you may lose them, or at least lose touch with them, perhaps, for always.

presents." In the largest study every done on adolescents (*Family Magazine,* March 1982) in which over 160,000 teens across the country were interviewed, youth of both sexes agreed by more than three to one that it's much easier to communicate and to get along with their mothers. Unless a father makes a strong effort to communicate with his kids when they are very young, it's almost impossible for him to initiate a close relationship when they are teenagers.

It is so easy to fool ourselves and be blinded to the facts, dad, about our relationship with our children. A survey by Michigan State University found that 79 percent of parents thought they communicated well with their children, while 81 percent of the *same* kids said their parents did not communicate with them. (*Dads Only,* quoted from *Christian Medical Society Journal,* March 1978.)

One survey of 130 executives found that while 48 percent claimed their families were their major interest in life, 63 percent said they would work late rather than go home. *Christianity Today* reported that a study in a small U.S. community showed the average time per day fathers spend with their very young sons is about thirty-seven seconds (May 12, 1979). One family life specialist found that the three things fathers say most in responding to their kids are: "I'm too tired," "We don't have enough money," and "Keep quiet."

I nearly cheered out loud a few years ago when I read, on the other hand, the comment of Dr. George Anderson on refusing the presidency of the Lutheran Church in America. He said, "We could have worked out the details of the job, but the issue is how close I can be with my children in the next few years. They are not a responsibility, they are a joy to me. At this age, they start talking to you, sharing what they think, and I don't want to miss it" (*Dads Only,* October 1978).

We live in an interesting and challenging era for dads. Psychologists and sociologists are churning out the reports on the vital importance of dads being at home and spending time with their children; the rise in working mothers is accentuating this emphasis. Recently, I seem to be seeing more and more editorials about the problems of too few fathers. And yet the divorce rate is higher than ever before, resulting in the legal separation of dads from their children more than ever. Many of our social problems are related to paternal deprivation, including homosexuality.

Ever more tragic, however, is the current chic trend of single women becoming impregnated in order to have children of their own without the baggage of a father. Ellen Goodman wrote movingly of this recently in an editorial.

If we dads can see ourselves as God's appointed servants in our homes, it will go a long way in helping us become respected by the whole family as the head.

A servant is one who gives and gives and gives. The picture of God providing for his children in the first few chapters of Genesis shows us *how* we are to give to our children. We give them life through conception (Genesis 2:7). We give them a home that is as lovely as we can make it (Genesis 2:8). We give them food (Genesis 2:9a), responsibility and work to do (Genesis 2:15). We must give them guidelines and explain to them in advance the consequences of disobedience and follow through if they disobey (Genesis 2:16–17). But, note in Genesis 3:21, we are, like God, to show mercy. We are to be concerned that they have good friendships (Genesis 2:18) and encourage their creativity (Genesis 2:19). We must ultimately allow them to make their own choices (Genesis 3) and experience the results (Genesis 3:22ff).

All this is not to say that headship does not involve any sort of initiatory leadership on your part, dads. It is my firm conviction that we fathers ought, and *can* (since what God desires, He will enable) take major initiative in family matters, particularly in matters related to our life with Christ. In his book *Passive Men, Wild Women* (Ballantine, 1983), Pierre Mornell quotes from Carl Jung:

> The libido of the American male is focused almost entirely upon his business so that as a husband, he is glad to have no responsibilities. He gives complete direction of his family life over to his wife. This is what you call giving independence to the American woman. It is what I call the laziness of the American man. (p. 44)

Dad should often be the one to lead in family Bible reading and family prayers. Dad should be the one to take the lead in seeing to it that the family is in church on Sundays. Dad should assume the responsibility to initiate conversations with the children about matters of personal faults and personal values. If these responsibilities are ignored by the father and completely taken up by the mom, it is quite possible that the child will assume that religion, etc. is "just for women" and not important to men. We dads must work at being as *close* to our children as their mothers are.

Newsweek reported an interesting finding that children who are close to their fathers, who are frequently cuddled and cared for by their dads, not only grow up to be more adaptable, and better able to withstand stress, but they also appear even to learn more easily. (*Dads Only,* March 1982; quoted from *Newsweek,* November 30, 1981). In the words of The Rev. Jesse Jackson, "Your children need your presence, more than your

Being head, moreover, does not guarantee that the father will always be respected. St. Paul exhorts wives to "respect their husbands" (Ephesians 5:33), and children always to "obey their fathers" (Ephesians 6:1), but this sort of respect comes naturally only when the man treats his family with respect as well (I Peter 3:7).

What the Bible means by headship, I believe, relates to the *manner* in which Christ loves his Church. "Husbands, love your wives as Christ loved the church and gave himself up for her" (Ephesians 5:25).

Several years ago, we were on a family vacation. I was exhausted and wanted only to sleep, eat and read. It had been an incredible year and I was "entitled to my rest." For some months previous, in our church, we had been emphasizing the idea of "servanthood," and I had served and served and served. Now, I just wanted to rest. It soon became apparent that our vacation was not going well. The kids were cranky and my wife kept asking me to give her some help. It didn't occur to me that *she* might need a vacation, too. Finally, things came to a head and I pulled one of my "spiritual" tricks by announcing that I had to get off alone and have a Quiet Time with God. I opened the Bible to read and my eyes fell on this very verse: "Love your wives as Christ loved the Church and *gave himself up for her.*" I had never really noticed this last phrase and it made me rather uncomfortable in light of the situation. "Lord," I said, "do you mean I have to be a servant in my own *home,* too?" Just as distinctly as if it were spoken aloud, I "heard" the response: "Yes, Yates. In fact, being a servant *starts* in your home. If you can't serve there, you may as well forget it."

Being head of the house means loving my family as Christ loved us. Loving in that way means being a servant to your family, not just when it's convenient, but always. Paul sums this up in this second verse, which I call to your attention:

"Do nothing out of selfish ambition or vain conceit, but in humility, consider others better than yourselves. Each of you should look not only to your own interest, but also the interests of others" (Philippians 2:3–4).

A husband and father must love without selfishness, in humility, and in an attitude of sacrifice and self-giving. This does not come naturally for any of us. We dads must constantly confess to God our own selfishness and self-importance and ask His help that we be more like Christ who gave up all His privileges and glory to serve. Because He loved us, He identified with us completely. So must we work very hard to put ourselves into the shoes of our mates or our children and, therefore, better understand their concerns.

whether to conduct your life in pursuit of money, status, power . . . or something else. The *something else* is hard to describe, because it's not part of the official story of my generation of women. But I know it's there.

I agree, the "something else" *is* hard to describe, but let me attempt it.

We have stressed in this study the need for husbands and wives to *share* in the parenting responsibilities. Yes, we need dads to spend time at home with our children—we need fewer absentee dads, but we don't need to combat that with absentee mothers. God has made mothers in such a way as to be crucial to the nurture of their children. A mother can give a child something which a dad cannot give, and I'm worried that the children of these "successful women" are being deprived of that something.

Fallows expresses her fears as a working mother:

I would love to humor him at these moments, to let him sleep late on overcast mornings, to let him play with his trucks and dawdle over his breakfast; but there is not time. I must be at my job before 9:00, which means we must leave the house before 8:30, which means he must start moving by 7:30 without fail. Certainly some of his balking is part of being two years old, and certainly he would do many of these things whether or not I worked. But I can't help feeling that my decision to work full-time this year has something to do with it. A child seems to sense unerringly when he is being rushed, when there's something on mommy's mind other than reading him a book or helping him assemble his train. Sometimes a child must be rushed, but I hate the thought of rush becoming the norm, replacing the sense that the child's parents have all the time and love in the world to give.

The imprint a woman makes on her family's lives is personal and private and not even much valued by the world beyond those few affected. A mother's efficiency and organization in running a household isn't particularly noticed (it's expected, taken for granted), but the care she puts into it is. To me, this means things like keeping our family tradition. . . . It's a presence that is not always noticed but would be missed if it were not there, providing the things that make up so many of the memories of one's own childhood. In these things, there is no substitute for time and a mother's touch.

The "successful woman" usually has simply underrated the value of these sorts of things because she has had to give them up. It is not possible to have it all. A woman simply cannot pursue, full-speed ahead, the prescribed course for the superwoman and at the same time nurture her children in all the ways a child needs. The pity is that in the high-style, intellectual and successful circles of American cities, there is, according to Fallows:

> a narrow-mindedness, ignorance, condescension, and indifference about motherhood. The people we meet at parties don't know what it means to be a successful mother, but they know about the achievements a successful woman can list. They don't know about people like my neighbor, a woman my own age with two children, who works as hard as any superachieving young lawyer or TV producer. Her son (about one year old) rises before 5:00 every morning, and her daughter (almost four) does not go to bed until 9:00. In between, they nap at different times, so that one of them is always up. She has no company-dictated coffee breaks or business lunches; nor does she have any outside measures of the quality and devotion of her work. Twenty years from now, her children may remember if she sews that Halloween costume or takes them sledding on the first snowy day, if she helps them put together puzzles instead of turning on the cartoons, if she tolerates "helping" hands when making the birthday cake and deals with the broken eggs and spilled milk later on. But these count for nothing in the measure of a modern woman's success.

For so many years we have measured the success of a man in terms of his career so that he almost has no choice nowadays but to pursue that course in life. But now, we are beginning to make the same mistake with women, measuring them in the same way. If a woman's success is only to be judged by her performance at work alone, this is no more sensible than the triviality of the standards of a beauty contest.

Mothers, I believe, need more of a sense of security in their calling just to be mothers. Mothering *is* an occupation, a calling. As little ones come along, how well a woman handles the increasing demands depends, at least in part, on her sense of personhood.

Gladys Hunt, writing in *Christianity Today* (May 1980), says of this:

> It is hard to imagine a calling more important than to help a child grow, to make him aware of his world, and to have an uncommon delight in goodness, truth, and beauty—and to have an uncommon commitment to them. In the final analysis, we cannot *make* our children; that is God's business. We can, however, provide a diet he can use. Mothers who do this best are themselves growing, delighted by their own potential and by others.

It is this delight that inspires poetic verse about motherhood. It inspires a football player to smile and say, "Hi, Mom. I love you," when the television camera suddenly zooms in on him on the bench. It inspires young children clutching coins in hot, sticky hands, to comb the variety store looking for the just-right gift for a mother too wonderful for what is found. It makes sentimental verse beautiful, not maudlin; for everyone, deep down, wants this kind of mother.

What a safe, beckoning place such a mother makes! I remember coming home from school, opening the door, and calling, "Mom!" I wouldn't have said I needed her; I only wanted to know she was there. My mother: she listened to my tales, showed me how to tear out the stitches and begin again, stayed up late at night to finish the dress I'd hoped to wear the next day, suggested I solve my problems in one way or another. So many memories crowd in. She was not a preaching mother, but a *being* mother, quicker to think of others than of herself.

There is an inexplicable bond of tenderness between mother and child that goes back to the first bonding between them in the womb. Children can learn to bond to others, a big sister, a nurse, etc., and a father can cultivate this sort of relationship also, but I believe a child needs his mother to be available. Recently a number of mothers in our church participated in a panel at an all-day women's retreat. All of them were older and their children nearly grown. I was impressed that, to a one, they all felt very strongly the importance of having been at home with their children when they were young. Each cited specifically the value of being in the house when the child arrived home after school. All these women have now entered the job market quite happily, but refused to do so when their children were younger. While there *are* many hints on how to establish effective guidelines for "latch-key kids" who come home to an empty house, this system has, as yet, not been able to demonstrate that it does not adversely affect the emotional well-being of children. In our own community, unattended kids, roaming the town after school, are becoming a serious problem.

For some parents there is no option about mom working. This is just an economic fact of life. For others there *is* an option. I am writing particularly here to those of you who have the option to stay home with your children. While the challenges of the day-in and day-out caring for little ones at home are enormous, for most, I believe, so too are the rewards. What a thrill to be there when junior takes his first step or says his first word. What an incredible blessing to have intimate contact with one's child daily and to see those marvelous little changes occurring and to be able to guide and direct your child through the stages described earlier by Erikson. I worry about the children of working mothers. I am told by some working mothers (and I have read some studies) that they are happier, more fulfilled, and better mothers. I wonder, however, if this doesn't often have to do with the age of the children, as well as the hours the mother works. When children enter into the middle grades and high school years, in some ways it is even more important for mom to "be there" and lend an ear. Life becomes incredibly complicated and, at times, incomprehensible for teenagers. The more that parents are available and present to talk, to observe, to counsel, the better.

One mother, fairly indignant with the idea that mothers working outside the home might be less effective with their children, claimed to be a much happier mother since she had completed her doctorate and was now working at a nearby university. Upon questioning, I learned that her job is part-time, her children are in junior high, and she is always able, not only to see them off to school in the morning, but she is at home when they return from school. That is quite a different matter from the mother who goes back to her full-time job six months after the baby is born. This Ph.D. mom probably *is* happier and more fulfilled and one can only say "hurrah!"

"BUT WE CAN'T AFFORD FOR ONE NOT TO WORK!"

As our economy sputters and as our expectations as to life's "necessities" increase, I suppose it is inevitable that there will be more and more families in which both parents work. The Census Bureau estimates that at least two million children between the ages of seven and thirteen take care of themselves in the hours before and after school when adults in the family cannot be at home (*Family Circle,* February 24, 1981). Some estimates claim that 58 percent of the mothers of school-aged children are now working outside their homes. The explanation one usually hears is that "we can't afford to do otherwise" but, as I look at these parents growing old practically overnight under the dual stress of parenting and working full time, I *wonder* if it is really *always* true. Let's not condemn or sit in judgment on mothers who work, but please parents, be very careful that this is the right thing for your family. It may be. It may not be.

One couple, very dear to me, has recently been going through the traumas of these dual responsibilities, not because either of them wanted the mother to work, but because the mortgage had to be paid and it seemed that the only way to pay it was for the mother to take a nighttime nursing job. My questions are, "Is owning a house really all that important? Is it worth the multiple stress and strain produced by this situation?"

We should not imply that there are simple easy answers to such questions. There are not, but mothers contemplating entering the work force should be forewarned of the inevitable difficulties that will arise. For some time I have saved the following notes from a conversation with a dear young mother who was obviously under a great deal of stress related to working and parenting. She noted a number of factors:

> *Guilt:* A lot of forces tend to work together to help a working mother feel guilty about leaving her kids or about not participating in school activities to the extent that other mothers may do. The guilt varies in degree according to the age of the child since parents, in-laws and friends tend to show disapproval to a mother who leaves small children even if she is impelled to do so by real economic necessity. Working mothers also miss their children during the day and have a real longing that they must learn to deal with. Having to leave a sick child because you have used up all your sick leave and vacation time hurts any mother and often causes marital tension if the father has to take time off from his own work. (Most companies do not permit sick leave for the care of sick children, so mothers are forced to lie about their health—another guilt-inducing situation.)
>
> Many people have "attitudes" about working mothers, revealed in conversation, that tend to increase guilt feelings. There is an unconscious assumption among some people that working mothers are selfish and ego-centered and generally work purely for their own satisfaction or for luxuries. In fact, nine out of ten working mothers of my acquaintance would prefer to be with their children and work for such things as food, shelter and clothing, earning as much as half or more of the family income.
>
> One woman I know who works full time and has three kids was told by a neighbor: 'I'm only going to work part-time because *my* children are *my* first priority.' Implication is that children are not the first priority for the full-time working mother.
>
> Relatives often play a part in guilt. One older woman was extolling the merits of being at home with one's children when her daughter, a working mother, reminded her that she herself worked. Said the mother: 'Well, of course, you don't know how your children will turn out yet, do you?'
>
> Children themselves often inadvertently add to the guilt feelings by asking why their mothers can't come to school during the day or take part in field trips, or why Daddy has to be the one to stay home on the day they've thrown up.

Job Stress: Unless a job is satisfying and challenging, a person is just filling up time to make money. While this may work for awhile, most people feel a real need to use their talents and become frustrated and depressed by a dissatisfying job. To get challenging and satisfying jobs and work one's way up in an organization, often requires overtime, travel, additional schooling, and an assertive and decisive personality. Working mothers generally turn down jobs with travel or overtime or accept them with agonizing guilt. Often they feel that they shouldn't try for better jobs because these jobs will demand too much of their energies. By not trying for jobs they are really qualified for, working mothers can easily begin to feel incompetent and less capable than their non-married, non-mother counterparts in the work force.

Women in the workforce are rewarded for competing successfully with men. But working wives and mothers have to be particularly sensitive to the assertive and competitive aspects of their personalities because these are often sources of conflict at home. Promotions, raises and business success for women may also create competitive feelings at home with husbands who may be having less success in the workforce.

Time Stress: While it is acceptable for a man to come home from work, admit fatigue, and read the paper, it is absolutely forbidden for a working mother to do so. Mother must walk through the door ready to satisfy the needs of her family as if she had never been away. Kids have to be attended to immediately. Dinner has to be made, the kitchen cleaned up, husbands listened to and given emotional support. The panic to seek "quality time" with the family forces a working mother to suppress all her natural instincts to collapse. It also creates pressure to do more compensative activities than she would ever do if she were home—take on some extraordinary project, for example, that more sensible mothers at home, recognizing their limits and not wracked with guilt, refrain from.

Example: One day last week, Mother A got up at her usual 5:30 a.m., made the evening's dinner, spent a little time in prayer and Bible reading, made the family breakfast and lunches, then rushed to her carpool with a briefcast stuffed with construction paper. At noon, at her desk, she cut out 20 Cub Scout silhouettes, 10 flower outlines for corsages for mothers, 1 eagle, 1 liberty bell, the outlines for every letter in the word 'independence,' and a map of the United States. These were *some* of the materials needed for the crafts the Cubs would work on for their Blue and Gold Dinner. Stuffing the crafts in her briefcase, she went home, did the usual dinner and dishes routine, helped her son with his spelling test, and then typed out the parts for a skit for the Blue and Gold Dinner while her husband hurried off to a Den leaders' meeting. That Saturday, after getting up early and carting all the materials to the car for a 9:00 a.m. Den meeting (including flags, flag holders, sign-up sheets, all the little craft pieces, pencils, crayons, scissors, etc.), the boys passed judgment on the project: 'This,' they said, 'is yucch!'

It would be helpful if we all eliminated the "oughts" and "shoulds" from our relationships with other women and accepted their positions both inside and outside the home with respect and love. We shouldn't assume that working mothers are more selfish and more satisfied or more successful any more than we should assume that mothers who are able to stay home with their children are less selfish and successful. We need to be aware of our individual needs as people who hurt.

Husbands who live with working mothers need to develop a comparable concept of themselves as working fathers so that a marriage can evolve into a full working partnership. This can be a wonderful growing experience for men who go about it in the right spirit.

Where both husbands and wives work, each face the challenge of learning to be totally flexible, for the sake of the needs of the other, and to be prepared to develop some traditions which may be quite different from the more traditional homes in which they may have grown up.

Mothers of little ones, who *are* working outside the home, even perhaps *more* than at-home-mothers, need the regular encouragement and support of an ongoing fellowship group. Sadly, they are the last ones to take the time to join such a group because of these pressures already mentioned.

These mothers need our love, friendship, prayers, and help. These are truly trying times for mothers in our society. I offer the following suggestions for mothers, knowing that a father can only understand and help just *so* much:

1. Take time to be with God.
2. Pray on the run. Rely on God for strength, wisdom and guidance.
3. Make time to be with your husband.
4. Get an early start.
5. Plan ahead.
6. Think highly of your job as a mother.
7. Forget perfection. Be realistic about your limitations.
8. Learn from other mothers.
9. Don't become a slave to other people's ideas about childraising.
10. Don't try to do everything for your family.

11. Set up time-saving family habits that will help keep the house in order.

12. Attend church and church school regularly.

13. Help your children to get to know other folks outside your own family.

14. Be flexible.

15. Remember always, "This, too, shall pass."

MEETING AND DISCUSSION

At this meeting I suggest that you make plans for your concluding FLAG retreat for your entire families. Now, let me urge you *not* to drop this idea. This weekend will probably be more fun than anything else your FLAG group has done. Use your creativity and come up with thorough plans.

1. Discuss the objectives that you agree on for the weekend.

2. Decide what you want to do to accomplish these objectives and who will be responsible for what.

Use the Appendix outline of what one FLAG group did and some of their materials as a stimulus for your own planning. You will come up with many ideas that are better suited for you.

Afterword: Where Do We Go From Here?

During the course of your FLAG experiment, you certainly have not answered all your questions about the complexities of family life, neither have you exposed yourself to all the helpful material now available for inquiring Christian parents. Perhaps you and the other members of your group would like to continue meeting just as you have been doing and study some of the excellent books that are listed in Appendix C. If the fellowship has been good and your families have enjoyed each other, I encourage you to keep on meeting. If you don't want to meet as frequently, you could meet once a month, studying the same material, take turns reporting and leading the discussion. You might also want to plan further evenings, days or weekends with all the children involved as well.

Another suggestion is that you give serious thought to leading another FLAG group yourself. How fantastic it would be if every young parent in the church would share in this experience. You don't have to be an expert to draw people together.

Let me urge you, however you follow through on your FLAG experience, not to just put this manual aside now. Re-read it, and continue to discuss these things within your own family. God wants your family life to be strong and will help in strengthening it if you continue to seek his help in carrying out your responsibilities as a parent. It is his desire to: "turn the hearts of the fathers to their children and the hearts of children to their fathers." (Malachi 4:6)

APPENDICES

APPENDIX A

Guidelines for Leaders of a FLAG Group

WHAT IS A FLAG GROUP? WHY BEGIN ONE? HOW?

This book has developed out of my experience, first as a husband and parent, and second from my observations of families in the three churches I have served.

Parents want so much to be *good* parents, yet often lack the wisdom or experience to know how to handle the inevitable problems that arise in child rearing. As the mother of five, my wife has been telephoned countless times at all hours of the day and night by distraught mothers needing guidance and direction for everything from how to evaluate a cough to how to handle a teenager caught with drugs in his possession. Similarly, Susan and I have often turned to our parents and other older adults who have "been through it all" when we needed reassurance or encouragement.

Not so long ago in America, people were born, grew up, lived and died usually in the same area in which their family had always lived. There were always aunts and uncles, cousins and friends around to turn to for help in the challenge of raising a family. Not so, today. Very few of the people in our suburban Washington area have parents or relatives living nearby. Most have moved here from somewhere else and will move on in three or four years. For this reason, we work very hard to develop a sense of "family-ness" in The Falls Church—for the church is, as Sociologist Dennis Guernsey says, "A Family of Families" (in *A New Design for Family Ministry;* David C. Cook, 1984. This theme permeates the entire book). Out of this concern has evolved the ideas contained in this workbook. It is an attempt to bring parents together into a regular fellowship group with the goal of helping each other learn more of what it means to have Christian family life.

Hundreds of books have been written on Christian marriage, Christian parenting, Christian single-parenting, and so on, and many workbooks have been produced for an individual (or couple) to study. While I have benefited from many of these books, I nevertheless have felt that if we could just get parents together and talking about the challenges of marriage and of raising children, we not only could help people develop Christian friendships but we could also enable parents to benefit from the wisdom of other parents.

The writer of Proverbs says "iron sharpens iron and so one man sharpens the countenance of another" (27:17). My experience has been simply that when Christian men and women come together regularly for study and sharing, they strengthen, encourage, and teach one another. Although friendship is usually extolled (like motherhood), our modern, fast-paced world often discourages true friendship. Over and over again I have had men, in particular, tell me that they really had *no* close friends with whom they could share their deepest selves. Friendship is often associated with youth and adolescence, with most friendships generally petering out by the time of marriage. Adults often have many acquaintances but few close friends. Women sometimes seem better able to develop deep friendships than men. Many of us forget that we need each other.

Jesus had close friends. Paul did. Moses did. Friendship is an important part of God's design for us. There are significant differences between friends and acquaintances. With a friend you can be totally yourself with no need to cover up, for he/she accepts you just as you are. A friend supports you, although he does not necessarily agree with you. Friends give themselves to each other without seeking to control one another. Francis Bacon said, "A friend doubles a man's joy and cuts his sorrow in half." One certainly cannot have this sort of relationship with just anyone, but God will give us such relationships with a few if we seek them out.

It is to be hoped that your best friend is your mate, but couples need "couple friends" as well. My wife and I are always on the look-out for other couples with whom we both feel a spark of congeniality. For, although these relationships are rather rare, they are extraordinarily rewarding. My hope is that through the FLAG groups, more and more such friendships will develop. For the past several years we have participated in such groups, and I have developed the FLAG plan as a guide for others seeking to deepen their Christian friendships and at the same time learn more about Christian parenting.

In the pages of this book is outlined a course of study and discussion that should last for about twelve to fifteen weeks (or more if the group doesn't meet every week). Hopefully, this will be just the beginning of some rich friendships.

I strongly suggest that the group meet every week; meeting less frequently leaves too much time in between to effectively pick up the threads from the previous meetings. However, given the fast pace of our lives, you might decide to meet every other week. This will somewhat decrease the speed at which you are able to really begin to share deeply, but it may be the best a particular group can do. Under no circumstances should a FLAG group meet less than every other week. Twelve or thirteen people is probably the maximum that should participate if we are going to encourage all members to be actively involved.

As far as the composition of the group is concerned, we have found it best to have parents whose children are mostly still of junior high age or younger. Parents with teenage children will add an invaluable degree of experience to the group but probably will not "get" as much from the study as they will give. A grandparent or two might bring extra wisdom to the group and a single parent would not only help all the married couples grow in awareness and sensitivity to the unique challenges of single parenthood today, but also the single parent would find invaluable strength and support in the group. It is best to choose families whose children are roughly the same ages. (Note: Since it is crucial to the success of the group that all children participate in the activities designed for the entire family unit, the children should be involved in the decision about joining FLAG. If a family commits to FLAG, this means even the teenagers have the family outings on their calendars and participate.)

The basic aim of the FLAG group is two-fold: To learn more about God's plan for family life; and to benefit from the experience of others in how to carry out these Biblical principles of family living. Recently, a teenager from several hundred miles away telephoned me to discuss a problem she was having with her boyfriend. This points out a third benefit of a group such as we've been describing. If the parents plan some evenings and/or weekends to bring all the members of the families together, then the parents also get to know the *children* of their friends as well, and other long-term relationships may develop. This particular girl who telephoned is the daughter of dear friends of ours who participated with us in our first parents group several years ago. She was in grammar school then and the family has since moved away. But the point is that, through the evenings and outings which we shared as *families,* this girl developed a relationship with a Christian adult who cared about her.

Little children will enjoy the FLAG get-togethers immensely. One mother told me that her seven-year-old suggested all moving into a FLAG hotel or apartment complex so they could be together all the time! The need for such relationships today is desperate. Our children need models of Christian adults—they need to know Christian men and Christian women of all sorts, sizes, dispositions, and occupations. Our Christian friends can often provide an example or a listening ear to our children which we cannot give. Our children need to witness other Christian homes and marriages, both to broaden their thinking and to reassure them that their own family isn't the only one which is seeking to know and do God's will.

In light of all this, I encourage you to kick off your FLAG group with an overnight retreat after having met once to get organized. This retreat should be for parents only; later events will include the kids in a variety of activities suggested in the workbook.

BEGINNING YOUR FLAG GROUP

Before starting your FLAG group, compile a list of various persons you would like to participate in such a group and discuss it with your minister. His suggestions and insights might be quite valuable. Then start your group in the fall of the year.

If you plan to start your group in September, for instance, approach the people you hope will join you in the group during the summer and discuss the idea with them. It's important that they understand that this is a major commitment of time and energy, and that some overnights will be involved. It is preferable that you work out the schedule well in advance and give it to them so that they can study it prior to the first meeting. Also, it will be helpful to share these objectives with them so that they can clearly understand the purpose of the group.

FLAG OBJECTIVES

1. To become a close-knit, supportive fellowship group in which the members care for and pray for one another.

2. To develop a clearer understanding of biblical teaching on the Christian home—the relationships and roles of its members.

GUIDELINES FOR LEADERS OF A FLAG GROUP 141

3. To counsel one another in the "how-to's" of Christian family life, sharing from our own personal experiences.

4. To involve our children in several of our meetings or outings so that they can develop a better relationship with the members of the other families.

5. To share in the leadership as seems desirable with the hope that some members of the group will lead another FLAG group in the future.

THE LEADER'S GUIDE FOR THE FIRST MEETING

There are four major concerns for this first evening together.
 1. To get to know one another better.
 2. To agree on the purpose and disciplines of the group and to commit to a schedule.
 3. To make plans for the kick-off retreat.
 4. To seek God's guidance in the whole venture.

The following format is suggested:
 1. Spend forty-five minutes or so telling a little about ourselves.
    a. Name, other members of family. (Pass around a sheet for each to list the names and ages of each child and a hobby, as well as parents' names and telephone numbers at home and at work. The leader should later pass out copies to all participants.)
    b. My job or how I'm currently spending my time.
    c. Let each person choose a piece of paper from a hat and respond to one of the questions on the paper:

    Sheet 1: Name one adult who significantly affected your life and thinking as a youth and explain how (may or may not have been a parent).

    　　or

    Tell about one book you read which has significantly affected your life and why.

    Sheet 2: Describe for us one of the happiest moments in your life. Why was it so happy?

    　　or

    If you could do anything in the world, what would it be and why would you do it?
 2. Next, take twenty minutes or so to review the objectives and add to or rewrite them (having them up on newsprint will help). They may want to express their thoughts as to how they hope the group will be helpful to them and put these ideas on newsprint as well.

3. It's important for all to agree as to how the time at the meetings will be spent, and then stick to that agreement.

The following covenant has worked well for other groups:
   a. To meet from 8:00 to 9:45 PM sharp.
   b. To have completed assignments by the time of the meeting.
   c. No food except on special occasions. Hosts will provide coffee, other drinks.
   d. No children except on special family occasions (nursing babies excepted!)
   e. Sessions will consist of:
      i. Response to Bible study and readings.
      ii. Sharing "how I'm feeling about our family life and my role in it."
      iii. Discussing concerns.
      iv. Prayer.
      v. Let us agree that in our sessions we will be as open and honest as possible. Let's avoid criticism and maintain complete confidentiality. The leader must demonstrate these attitudes right away and consistently.
4. Agree on the nights that group will meet and also put any special outings or overnights on the calendar. (Assuming the overnight retreat is coming up soon, be sure all matters of directions, what to bring, etc., are covered.)
5. Finally, take a little while to join in prayer asking God's blessing and guidance, particularly remembering any special concerns for the group that may have arisen from the evening's discussion.
6. Assign the following Bible study, and "Why is it so tough to raise a family in our town," to be completed by the retreat.

BIBLE STUDY: PSALM 127

This psalm is attributed to Solomon and has perhaps a concealed signature in verse two with the term "beloved" which in Hebrew is *Jedediah*—the name given to Solomon by God (II Samuel 2:25). Sadly, like much of Solomonic wisdom, the lessons of this psalm, as pertinent as they were to his own situation, were eventually mostly lost on him. "His building, both literal and figurative, became reckless (I Kings 9:10 ff), his kingdom a ruin (I Kings 11:11 ff), and his marriages a disastrous denial of God (I Kings 11:1 ff)."*

*Kidner, Derek, Psalms *73-150,* Tyndale Old Testament Commentaries, IVP, 1975.

The psalm is in two parts, but both proclaim that only what is from God is really strong. The two senses of the word "house" (a dwelling or a family) are a well-known play on words in the Hebrew Old Testament—"builders" (verse one) is *bonim* and "sons" (verse three) is *banim*.

Read the psalm in two different versions:

Good News Bible

If the Lord does not build the house, the work of the builders is useless;
If the Lord does not protect the city, it does no good for the sentries to stand guard.
It is useless to work so hard for a living, getting up early and going to bed late.
For the Lord provides for those he loves while they are asleep.
Children are a gift from the Lord; they are a real blessing.
The sons a man has when he is young are like arrows in a soldier's hand.
Happy is the man who has many such arrows. He will never be defeated when he meets his enemies in the place of judgment (Psalm 127).

New American Standard Bible

Unless the Lord builds the house, they labor in vain who build it;
Unless the Lord guards the city, the watchman keeps awake in vain.
It is vain for you to rise up early, to retire late,
To eat the bread of painful labors;
For He gives to His beloved even in his sleep.
Behold children are a gift of the Lord;
The fruit of the womb is a reward
Like arrows in the hands of a warrior, so are the children of one's youth.
How blessed is the man whose quiver is full of them; They shall not be ashamed,
When they speak with their enemies in the gate.

1. Three of the most universal occupations are mentioned in this psalm; what would you say they are?

2. What are the two different attitudes described in the first half of verse 1?

3. Whatever we do in the area of building, creating, developing or conserving may be done with either of the above attitudes. If we do not see our work as being done in dependence upon God and ultimately for God, then what is the point of doing it? Is there a point according to Solomon?

4. How are children an example of what verse 2 is saying?

5. Psalm 127 might be said to be a commentary on the first and last paragraphs of Genesis 11 where man builds for glory and security, achieving only confusion, whereas God quietly gives to the obscure Terah a son in whom all the earth has been blessed. Look at these paragraphs in Genesis 11.

6. (Back to Psalm 127.) Why does the writer not mention things such as financial wealth and position in verses 3–5 as he describes family life?

7. Children are a gift from the Lord. Is it true of any of the gifts of God that at first they are responsibilities or liabilities before they become obvious assets? "The greater their promise, the more likely these sons will be a handful before they are a quiverful."

8. What do you think it means when it speaks of "the Lord" building the house?

9. How do you think we as parents are called to work at this task in partnership with God?

10. How can this group be an aid in the task of helping us to build true Christian family life? What do you hope to gain from this group?

GUIDELINES FOR LEADERS OF A FLAG GROUP

THE FIRST RETREAT

Because it takes time to get to know one another well, and because that kind of relationship will be a great aid in helping your FLAG group achieve its objective, a twenty-four-hour retreat is one of the best ways to bring everyone closer together at the start. It will be worth the effort involved in locating a place and working out all the necessary arrangements. I recommend going only an hour or less from home and spending from early Saturday morning through Sunday morning together. Or perhaps go on Friday night and return Saturday night or Sunday morning in time for church.

Here follows a suggested outline of activities (you should alter or amplify the schedule as appropriate):

9:00– 9:30	Coffee and donuts
9:30–10:00	Sharing our thoughts from the Bible study on Psalm 127
10:00–10:45	Quiet time where each person goes off on his own and does the Bible study for Psalm 78 (see following section)
10:45–11:30	Discussion of the Bible study
11:30–12:30	Continuation of the discussion

During this continuation, each group member should take twenty minutes to list quietly all the major qualities or values or lessons learned from parents. On a sheet of paper make one column for mothers and one for fathers and under each begin to list *any* of these qualities, convictions, attitudes, etc. learned from each parent. (If parents are not appropriate, then choose another important person.)

After you have made your lists, then identify each "learning" with either an "M" or a "T." "M" means you learned this because it was simply *modeled* by the parents and "T" means it was *taught*. "MT" means it was both modeled and taught.

Compute the total "learnings" from mother, from father.

How many were "M"?
How many were "T"?
How many were "MT"?

Do you see yourself as an "M" or "T" type teacher of your children? How do you see your spouse? How do you think your children would rate you? Your spouse?

Next, share these observations with your mate (if you are a single parent, share with one of the couples or other single.)

Finally, with your mate, list the major things you want to pass on to your own children and then together, as a group, let each couple share three to five of the most desired qualities to pass on and also tell what they learned from the exercise about how their *parents* taught them.

Take the afternoon as free time to do some group activities such as volleyball, hiking, picking apples, etc.

After dinner and clean-up, gather for another hour of sharing. After taking some time to think about it, let each person take ten minutes or so to express the most important turning points that led to our present level of commitment to Christ. An alternate suggestion is to have parents share where they think their family life is presently weak and strong.

Conclude the evening with an informal worship service, prayer time and singing.

BIBLE STUDY: PSALM 78:1-8

This psalm is said to have been written by Asaph, one of the descendants of Korah, a man who died in rebellion against God (Numbers 26:10ff). One part of Korah's descendants became guardians of the temple, another part became singers and musicians of the temple choir founded under David. Asaph was apparently both an inspired musician and poet. Twelve psalms are attributed to other members of this family and twelve to Asaph himself. Perhaps these were special songs sung by Asaph's choir.

Good News Bible

> Listen, my people, to my teaching, and pay attention to what I say.
> I am going to use wise sayings and explain mysteries from the past,
>   things we have heard and known, things that our fathers told us.
> We will not keep them from our children: we will tell the next
>   generation about the Lord's power and his great deeds and the
>   wonderful things he has done.
> He gave laws to the people of Israel and commandments to the
>   descendents of Jacob.
> He instructed our ancestors to teach his laws to their children, so that
>   the next generation might learn them and in turn should tell their
>   children.
> In this way they also will put their trust in God and not forget what
>   he has done, but always obey his commandments.

They will not be like their ancestors, a rebellious and disobedient
   people, whose trust in God was never firm,
And who did not remain faithful to him (Psalm 78:1–8).

New American Standard Bible

Listen, O my people, to my instructions;
Incline your ears to the words of my mouth.
I will open my mouth in a parable;
I will utter dark sayings of old,
Which we have heard and known,
And our fathers have told us.
We will not conceal them from their children
But tell to the generation to come the praises of the Lord,
And His strength and His wondrous works that He has done.
For He established a testimony in Jacob,
And appointed a law in Israel,
Which He commanded our fathers,
That they should teach them to their children:
That the generation to come right now, even the children
   yet to be born.
That they may arise and tell them to their children,
That they should put their confidence in God,
And not forget the works of God
But keep His commandments
And not be like their fathers,
A stubborn and rebellious generation,
A generation that did not prepare its heart,
And whose spirit was not faithful to God. (Psalm 78:1–8)

1. What qualities are attributed to God in these verses?

2. What do these qualities tell us about God's concerns for his people?

3. What role do parents play in the process described here by the psalmist?

4. Please list what you see (arising out of these verses) as the most important tasks of a parent in relationship to children.

5. Now add to this list other major tasks of a parent.

6. Reread both lists. How do they make you feel?

7. In which areas do you feel you most need help? What steps might you take to get that help?

AN EVENT FOR THE WHOLE FLAG FAMILY

At least once or twice between the first retreat (parents only) and the last one (which will include children as well) it is important to get all the families together for an evening or an afternoon. I suggest doing this as soon as possible. Only through events like this will the kids get to know the other adults in the FLAG group and vice versa. It may be that a gathering could be in connection with some special event such as someone's birthday, Thanksgiving, Valentine's Day, etc. If so, the plans for the evening could focus on one special event. Or there may be no special event at all. The major objectives for such an evening follow:

1. All ages are to have a good time so that kids and parents anticipate more such good times in the future.

2. Everyone is to get to know everyone else so that by the end of the evening we all know one another's names and something about them. A special, imaginative means of introduction can be quite affirming, to the younger ones especially.

3. The kids are to develop an idea as to what the FLAG group is.

4. We are to have intergenerational communication so that some relationships can begin to develop.

Here is one such plan you might want to follow.

6:00–6:30	Families arriving and arranging food for potluck supper.
7:15	Dessert all together in family room. As you are eating, you will introduce one another. Going around the circle, kids first introduce their parents, telling one funny or significant thing about that

GUIDELINES FOR LEADERS OF A FLAG GROUP

	parent. Then the parents introduce their children by telling one "brag" item, or something particularly good or special about each child.
8:00	After clearing the dishes, have everyone gather again while the leader explains to the children just what the FLAG group is. He might choose some poems or songs or a short story (such as "I am a Promise" by Bill Gaither or "Cats in the Cradle") to illustrate why the parents want to learn to be better parents. Then divide into family groups (at least two families per group) of roughly equal size, give everyone a paper and some crayons and ask each person to "create" a picture of "my family," a happy memory or one thing "I like best." Starting with the children, let each person explain their creation (still in small groups).
8:45	Now it's time to have some fun with a game and let the little ones show off. You might play a rowdy outdoor game like dodgeball, kick-the-can, or capture the flag, or some indoor game. It must be something that all ages can participate in—rules may have to be changed to allow the younger ones to participate.
9:20 or 9:30	All come together for a quiet closing. If you have a musician among you, you might sing some songs, or simply have some "thank you" prayers.

As a group, you may decide to do something completely different such as a family skit night or talent show, etc. The point is to plan an activity that will achieve these objectives which are described.

ONE GROUP'S NOTES FROM A
FLAG WEEKEND RETREAT FOR THE WHOLE FAMILY

Theme: God has a special plan for each person.

Study: Joshua

SCHEDULE

Saturday

10:00	Arriving at Yate's Farm
	Refreshments—Julie and Christine
	Games—Jackie
	Looking at Joshua
	1. John tells the story
	2. Quiet times—Barbara
	3. Sharing all together—Barbara
	4. Treasure Hunt—Jackie
12:30	Lunch—Julie and Christine
	A walk to the store—Roger
	Hiking—Dan
	Canoeing—Fred
	Other free time activities
3:00	Tea Party—Julie and Christine
3:30	Scavenger Hunt—Susan
	Free time activities
6:00	Supper—Jackie and Christine
	Setting up tents for kids—Roger
	Campfire—John
8:00	Campfire
	S'mores—Jackie and Christine
	Singing—Julie
	Family Sharing—John
10:00	Lights out

Sunday

8:00	Breakfast—Roger
10:00	Worship—Dan with older kids helping
12:00	Sandwiches available for those who stay for lunch

Note:

All kids and adults should bring Bible, paper and pen.
Christine and Julie think the cost for food for the weekend will come to about $5.00 per person. We can work that out this weekend.

GUIDELINES FOR LEADERS OF A FLAG GROUP

FLAG RETREAT GOALS

1. Children develop closer relationship with some of the FLAG parents.
2. Our families grow closer together in sharing and praying for one another.
3. Joyful time of worship for all.
4. Memorable fun and recreation together.
5. To study a biblical theme throughout the weekend.

GETTING-TO-KNOW-YOU GAME

Everyone writes down on a piece of paper three things about themselves such as favorite hobby, what you like to do in your spare time, are you an indoor or outdoor person, what do you like to do, something that is very important in your life, or where you were born. These pieces of paper will be collected and put in a hat. Each person draws a slip of paper, reads it and tries to guess who it is.

GETTING-TO-KNOW-YOU QUESTION

What do you love most about the person in your family who is the next younger in line behind you.

PROCEDURE FOR TREASURE HUNT

1. Divide FLAG group into groups of four people (two adults, two children and not from the same family, if possible).
2. Color-code each group.
3. Select tangible items to be the treasures from whichever Bible story is to be the central focus of the weekend.
4. Give each group six treasures to find.
5. Look around the house or buy very inexpensive things (at the "dime" store) to represent the selected treasures from the Bible story.
6. Put the treasures in clear zip-lock-type sandwich bags.
7. Punch a hole and tie a ribbon through the corner of the bag. (You can use inexpensive strings from a bag of hoops for making pot holders.) The color of the ribbon should match the color of the group looking for that particular treasure.
8. Hide the treasures.
9. Make up and hand out "clues" about the treasure (What did Rahab tie in her window?) as well as where the treasure might be found (Look near the lilac tree).
10. Let the children keep the treasures.

GROUP 1—THE RED GROUP

Find:

A tool that *modern day* spies might use.
   (Hint: Look near the lilac trees.)
Material that Rahab used to cover the spies.
   (Hint: Look in the barn.)
The special sign that Rahab tied in her window.
   (Hint: Look in the high window.)
The number of days the spies hid in the mountains before reporting back to Joshua.
   (Hint: Look around the raspberries.)
A picture of what the Israelites slept in.
   (Hint: Look around the mailbox.)
A type of food that God provided for the Israelites once they entered Canaan.
   (Hint: Look around the woodsy horse trail.)

Remember:

Leave anything that is not in a bag with your team color. Don't give it away to the other teams where their "treasures" are hidden if you happen to find them.

(Answers: binoculars, flax, red cord, three days, tent, vegetable.)

GROUP 2—THE BLUE GROUP

Find:

What spies used to lower themselves down from Rahab's window.
   (Hint: Look around the trees in the little yard.)
What God parted to allow the Israelites to cross over into Canaan.
   (Hint: Look around where the fish swim.)
What Joshua told twelve men to take from the riverbed.
   (Hint: Look around the front entrance.)
Something that "flowed" into Canaan.
   (Hint: Look around the future tree house.)
Something else that "flowed" in Canaan.
   (Hint: Look in the mint patch.)

GUIDELINES FOR LEADERS OF A FLAG GROUP 153

What the Israelites marched around thirteen times.
  (Hint: Look around the volleyball court.)

Remember:

Leave anything that is not in a bag with your team color. Don't give it away to the other teams where their "treasures" are hidden if you do happen to find them.

(Answers: rope, Jordan River, twelve large stones, milk, honey, walls of Jericho.)

GROUP 3—THE PURPLE GROUP

Find:

The first thing that the priests carried across the Jordan River.
  (Hint: Look at the chapel site.)
Something the Israelites ate when they first got to Canaan.
  (Hint: Look around the stable.)
What the priests blew as the Israelites marched around Jericho.
  (Hint: Look at the head of the creek.)
Something the Israelites destroyed once they entered city of Jericho.
  (Hint: Look at the head of the creek.)
Something that Achan stole.
  (Hint: Look around the horse jump.)
Something else that Achan stole.
  (Hint: Look along the woodsy horse trail.)

Remember:

Leave anything that is not in a bag with your team color. Don't give it away to the other teams where their "treasures" are hidden if you do happen to find them.

(Answers: The Ark of the Covenant, parched corn, trumpets, cattle, silver, coat.)

GROUP 4—THE YELLOW GROUP

Find:

What Joshua set up in the middle of the Jordan riverbed.
   (Hint: Look near the swings.)
Something the Israelites ate when they had settled in Canaan.
   (Hint: Look around the woodsy horse trail.)
Something that grew in abundance in Canaan.
   (Hint: Look around the stable.)
Something the Israelites destroyed once they entered the city of Jericho.
   (Hint: Look around the horse jump.)
Something the Israelites found among the ruins of Jericho.
   (Hint: Look around the front gate.)
Something that God made stand still during the battle of Gibeon.
   (Hint: Look around the "cigar" tree.)

Remember:

Leave anything that is not in a bag with your team color. Don't give it away to the other teams where their "treasures" are hidden if you happen to find them.

(Answers: twelve stones, bread, grain, sheep, silver coins, sun.)

GROUP 5—THE GREEN GROUP

Find:

A type of food that grew in abundance in Canaan.
   (Hint: Look around the apple trees.)
A weapon used by the Israelites.
   (Hint: Look near the big pond tree.)
Something the Israelites found among the ruins of Jericho.
   (Hint: Look around the horse jump.)
Something that Achan stole.
   (Hint: Look around the swings.)
Something that God caused to fall on the Gibeonites which threw them into a panic.
   (Hint: Look around the lilac trees.)
What Old Testament writers such as Joshua used to write on in place of a book.
   (Hint: Look around the "cigar" tree.)

GUIDELINES FOR LEADERS OF A FLAG GROUP

Remember:

Leave anything that is not in a bag with your team color. Don't give it away to the other teams where their "treasures" are hidden if you do happen to find them.

(Answers: fruit, sword, gold, gold bar, hailstones, scrolls.)

GOD HAS A PLAN (MISSION) FOR YOU!
A BIBLE STUDY IN JOSHUA FOR BIG KIDS

1. Pray for God to teach you something special.
2. Read Joshua Chapter 1.
3. Answer the following questions:
   a. God gives Joshua a specific mission here. List the specific things Joshua must do and be to fulfill God's mission.
   b. How does what God called Joshua to be apply to my life?
   c. What two promises does God make Joshua in Chapter 1?
   d. How do these promises apply to me?
   e. Think of a specific time in the coming week you might need to remember these promises.
   f. What was the people's response to Joshua's command?
   g. What should my response be to God in my life?
4. Memorize Joshua 1:9, Joshua 24:15

The greatness of a person's power is the measure of his surrender. It is not a question of who you are or of what you are, but whether God controls you.

—Henrietta Mears

Reward: It's not the amount of faith that matters but the object of my faith.
1. How did Joshua prove that he was trustworthy and faithful enough to be used by God to lead His people? Numbers 13:16–20 and 14:5–10
2. Why did God repeatedly insist that Joshua and the Israelites slay all of the people whom they conquered? Exodus 23:31–33
3. Why did God command twelve stones to be taken from the bed of the Jordan river after the Israelites had crossed over? Joshua 4:1–7
4. What "stones of memorial" do you have to remind you of what God has done in your life? List them to hang on to when you face difficulties.

GOD HAS A PLAN (MISSION) FOR YOU!
A BIBLE STUDY IN JOSHUA FOR MIDDLE KIDS

1. Pray for God to teach you something special.
2. Read Joshua Chapter 1.
3. Answer the following questions:
    a. God gives Joshua a specific mission here. List the specific things Joshua must do and be to fulfill God's mission.
    b. How does what God called Joshua to be apply to my life?
    c. What two promises does God make Joshua in Chapter 1?
    d. How do these promises apply to me?
    e. Think of a specific time in the coming week you might need to remember these promises.
    f. What was the people's response to Joshua's command?
    g. What should my response be to God in my life?
4. Memorize Joshua 1:9, Joshua 24:15

The greatness of a person's power is the measure of his surrender.
It is not a question of who you are or of what you are, but whether God controls you.

—Henrietta Mears

Reward: It's not the amount of faith that matters but the object of my faith.

ACTIVITIES FOR YOUNG CHILDREN
DURING ADULT QUIET TIME

1. Act out, using either the children or toys, one important aspect of the Bible story.
2. Make a scroll in advance for each child (you can use dowels and the widest adding-machine tape available). They can use these scrolls to draw their favorite part of the Bible story or to write out and illustrate their favorite Bible verse. Share these scrolls in the small group and again when the big group gets back together.

APPENDIX B

Divorce and Remarriage for Christians

Because divorce is such a major factor in family breakdown today, we must look carefully at the issue from a Christian perspective. Each year the number of divorces increases proportionately compared to the number of marriages. In 1940 there was one divorce for every six marriages; by 1960 the ratio was 1 to 4;[1] now in our day there is a corresponding divorce for every marriage. When asked about marriage, a young actress said in 1983:

> I do think about it. . . . I think about children more than I think about getting married. Not children—one child. But not for a long time. I'm too young. I haven't finished having fun. But I'm sure I will. I'm sure I'll get divorced too. Why not? You've got to do it once. Everyone seems to.[2]

Unquestionably, almost every Christian home is affected by this current phenomenon in family breakdown, and pastors are confronted regularly with married persons desiring to be divorced and with divorcees desiring remarriage. Clergy spend hours and hours meeting with these people, seeking to guide them, and in hardly any area is there more disagreement among Christians as to just exactly what God does teach us regarding divorce and remarriage. It is quite clear, from our look at marriage thus far, that God intends marriage to be permanent. God hates divorce. It is not within his perfect plan. However, sin has infected the human race and the church as well and although God's perfect will did not include divorce, the presence of sin in the world has brought about the reality of divorce as well as remarriage. We see in Deuteronomy 24 that God allowed for the toleration of divorce and remarriage. What does the New Testament teach? Let us look first at Mark 10:1-12.

> And he left there and went to the region of Judea and beyond the Jordan, and crowds gathered to him again; and again, as his custom was, he taught them.
>
> And Pharisees came up and in order to test him asked, "Is it lawful for a man to divorce his wife?" He answered them, "What did Moses command you?" They said, "Moses allowed a man to write a certificate of divorce, and to put her away." But Jesus said to them, "For your hardness of heart he wrote you this commandment. But from the beginning of creation, 'God made them male and female. . . . For this reason a man shall leave his father and mother and be joined to his wife, and the two shall become one. So they are no longer two but one. What therefore God has joined together, let not man put asunder.' "
>
> And in the house the disciples asked him again about this matter. And he said to them, "Whoever divorces his wife and marries another commits adultery against her; and if she divorces her husband and marries another, she commits adultery."

Divorce was accepted by virtually all Jews in Jesus' day based on the regulation of Deuteronomy 24:1-4:

> When a man takes a wife and marries her, if then she finds no favor in his eyes because he has found some indecency in her, and he writes her a bill of divorce and puts it in her hand and sends her out of his house, and she departs out of his house, and if she goes and becomes another man's wife, and the latter husband dislikes her and writes her a bill of divorce and puts it in her hand and sends her out of his house, or if the latter husband dies, who took her to be his wife, then her former husband, who sent her away, may not take her again to be his wife, after she has been defiled; for that is an abomination before the Lord, and you shall not bring guilt upon the land which the Lord your God gives you for an inheritance.

There was great disagreement as to what the legitimate causes for divorce might be. Jesus makes the following points: *First,* Moses permitted divorce due to man's sinfulness, not because divorce is right. *Second,* God's plan for marriage was that it be a permanent unity. Man should not seek to break apart what God decrees shall be joined. A good paraphrase of Mark 10:9 is, "Stop severing marriage unions which God has permanently bound together."[3] *Third,* to divorce and remarry another is to commit adultery against the first. In other words, legal divorce (legal according to Moses law) still does not dissolve the first marriage.

St. Luke reaffirms this teaching in chapter 16:18.

> Everyone who divorces his wife and marries another commits adultery, and he who marries a woman divorced from her husband commits adultery.

In turning to Matthew's gospel, we find that his account of Jesus' teaching is slightly different from Mark and Luke. There are two pertinent passages:

> It was also said, "Whoever divorces his wife, let him give her a certificate of divorce." But I say to you that everyone who divorces his wife, except on the ground of unchastity, makes her an adulteress, and whoever marries a divorced woman commits adultery (Matt 5:31–32).
>
> And Pharisees came up to him and tested him by asking, "Is it lawful to divorce one's wife for any cause?" He answered, "Have you not read that he who made them from the beginning made them male and female, and said, 'For this reason a man shall leave his father and mother and be joined to his wife, and the two shall become one'? So they are no longer two but one. What therefore God has joined together, let no man put asunder." They said to him, "Why then did Moses command one to give a certificate of divorce, and to put her away?" He said to them, "For your hardness of heart Moses allowed you to divorce your wives, but from the beginning it was not so. And I say to you: whoever divorces his wife, except for unchastity, and marries another, commits adultery" (Matt 19:3–9).

Here Jesus is making essentially the same points as those recorded by Mark and Luke except that now Jesus allows one exception, that of "unchastity." The disciples seem to understand Jesus to be saying essentially that divorce is not an option since their own response (vs. 10) is basically "If you can't get out of a marriage when you want to, then perhaps it would be better not to marry at all." "The disciples said to him, 'If such is the case of a man with his wife, it is not expedient to marry' " (Matt 19:10). Jesus then goes on to discuss the single life, as we have already seen.

So now Jesus is giving an out, the exception clause, "except for unchastity." Some argue that this clause is not a part of the actual teaching of Jesus; however there appear to be no sound arguments against the genuineness of the text.[4] The question then becomes "What does unchastity mean?" The word in Greek is *porneia,* which is derived from the noun *porne.* This comes from the root "to sell," hence implying an idea of offering one's body for a price. *Porneia* therefore came to refer to marital unfaithfulness and unlawful sexual intercourse. It is translated variously as unchastity, fornication, prostitution and adultery. It can also refer to sexual aberrations (Rom 1:29) and to incest (1 Cor 5:1). Exactly what Jesus meant when he offered this one exception is unclear and scholars are quite divided on the topic.

The general interpretations: *One,* some say Jesus meant simply adultery or unlawful sexual intercourse, implying that intercourse with a person other than one's spouse breaks the one flesh relationship with one's spouse. There is, however, another Greek word which even more explicitly refers to adultery—*moicheia*—and it seems that this word would have been more precise had he been referring simply to sexual unfaithfulness in marriage; *Two,* others say Jesus was referring to unfaithfulness during the betrothal period. Although Jewish betrothal was as binding as marriage, if the betrothed was guilty of sexual infidelity during the betrothal period and this was discovered prior to or on the wedding night, a lawsuit could be filed and the partner released from the marriage. Joseph's plan to quietly set aside the marriage to Mary, when she was discovered to be pregnant, is an example of this principle (Matt 1:19), but Jesus and the Pharisees do not appear to have been discussing betrothal but rather marriage. *Three,* another theory relates Jesus' teaching to marriage to a Gentile idolator. This idea is based on the Old Testament examples of Ezra (9 and 10) and Nehemiah (13:23–31) in which they demanded that those Jews who had married outside their faith divorce their wives. These occurrences, however, seem to have been rather unique, and St. Paul (1 Cor 7) teaches that Christians should remain married to their unbelieving spouse.

Four, still others say that *porneia* refers to an incestuous marriage relationship as described in Leviticus 18:6–18. It was against Jewish law to marry a near relative, and *porneia* may certainly be used for such an incestuous relationship. Incestuous marriages were rather popular among political leaders of Jesus' day; in fact, it was in denouncing such a relationship that John the Baptist was beheaded. It is clearly possible that Jesus was saying that only in a situation where a person had been unlawfully joined in marriage to a relative, was divorce acceptable.[5]

One wishes that we could be more certain as to the clear meaning of Jesus in this exception clause. Divorce is allowed, according to Moses and Jesus, under certain conditions but it is clearly contrary to the perfect will of God. It does seem clear that remarriage was allowed under the

Deuteronomic law and that is the case of the one allowable exception given by Jesus in Matthew. The Lord assumes the person will remarry; the remarriage is described as adulterous unless the union of the first marriage was broken by *porneia*. *Porneia* was the just cause for legal dissolution of marriage and constituted a splitting asunder whether the legal divorce document was enacted or not.

Now we move on to St. Paul who adds to the discussion in dealing with specific questions raised by the Corinthian church.

> To the married I give charge, not I but the Lord, that the wife should not separate from her husband (but if she does, let her remain single or else be reconciled to her husband), and that the husband should not divorce his wife.
>
> To the rest I say, not the Lord, that if any brother has a wife who is an unbeliever, and she consents to live with him, he should not divorce her. If any woman has a husband who is an unbeliever, and he consents to live with her, she should not divorce him. (1 Cor. 7:10–13)

The following points may be made: One, married Christians should not seek divorce. Two, if a divorce or separation occurs, they should either remain single or be reconciled. Paul does not comment on any exception to this rule presumably because the woman in question did not have a valid ground for divorce. This was not an example of *porneia*. If it had been, one would assume that Paul would not have said categorically "remain unmarried" since Jesus had already taught that *porneia* breaks asunder a marriage. Then Paul goes on to say: "But if the unbelieving partner desires to separate, let it be so; in such a case the brother or sister is not bound. For God has called us to peace (vs 15)."

In this case a believer is married to an unbeliever. The unbeliever desires to separate. We believe this means divorce as it is the same word quoted by Matthew in Matthew 19:6, "Let not man put asunder." The believer should not contest the divorce as he is called to be peaceful in all things. Paul does not comment on remarriage in such an instance, and scholars disagree as to whether marriage would have been allowed in such a situation. If the person is "not bound" there is good reason to suggest that the person is therefore loosed from the marriage partner and not bound to him in any way. Guy Duty, in commenting on this, states, "He or she was free to remarry. If they could not remarry, they certainly were in bondage, were they not?"[6]

Many church fathers, Martin Luther, Protestant commentators of the sixteenth and seventeenth centuries, Bishop Lightfoot, Archbishop Fisher,

Deissmann, and countless other historic scholars agree. Protestant commentators have usually taken this line of interpretation. For example, the divorce . . . it would seem, authorizes a remarriage since the believer ceases to be bound; his previous marriage is now disqualified.[7]

On the other hand, more conservative scholars would agree with the following conclusion,

> If an unbelieving husband divorces his wife, she is no longer bound to her husband, but she is still bound to the law of God. The freedom of a deserted believer does not imply the freedom to marry. The two alternatives of reconciliation or a lifelong single life would still apply.[8]

Later on in the same chapter, St. Paul addressed the unmarried:

> Now concerning the unmarried, I have no command of the Lord, but I give my opinion as one who by the Lord's mercy is trustworthy. I think that in view of the impending distress it is well for a person to remain as he is. Are you bound to a wife? Do not seek to be free. Are you free from a wife? Do not seek marriage. But if you marry, you do not sin, and if a girl marries she does not sin. Yet those who marry will have worldly troubles, and I would spare you that (7:26–28).

The statement "are you free [loosed] from a wife? Do not seek marriage. But if you marry, you do not sin . . ." refers, according to some, to a divorced person (as in verse 15) yet others feel this applies only to those who have never married.

From just this brief look at some of the more relevant New Testament passages dealing with divorce and remarriage, we see that theologians are unable to come to agreement as to the precise interpretation of these words. Still, the overall New Testament teaching is unified. God desires that couples marry and not divorce. Although there are certain situations in which divorce is allowable, permanence in marriage is preferable. In the case of "unchastity" or of permanent dissolution of the marriage by the other party, divorce is allowable but forgiveness and reconciliation is always possible.

Since there are certain situations in which a marriage partner will sin against the spouse to the degree that divorce is allowable, it therefore becomes a matter of judgment as to whether a particular person may be remarried. Sometimes the judgment is simple; usually, however, it is quite difficult to make. Some solve the problem simply by saying they will never approve of a remarriage. This, however, does not seem acceptable.

In the face of persistent streams of persons coming to church today with questions about these matters, I believe we can make the following points.

CONCLUSION

God's ideal plan does not include divorce. His desire is that we become partners and serve one another all our lives. Man, however, is sinful. Because of this, marital happiness is often broken. In some cases, marriages die. Sometimes they are put to death by adultery or other sexual infidelity such as homosexuality. Sometimes they are split asunder by persistent mental adultery. A husband may become preoccupied with lustful thoughts toward others and have no physical contact with his wife. Jesus taught us that sin is conceived inside a person and the sin is sin whether it is actually physically enacted or not. A person's thought life can be as condemning as his deeds and just as paralyzing in its negative results. A person's heart can become hardened against his mate, refusing to accept his responsibility to love and cherish his mate. A person can so physically and psychologically abuse his spouse, or so actively detest his mate, as to constitute "murder in the heart" and to make the continuation of life together unthinkable. Marriages can be killed in many ways.

For such reasons, God has allowed divorce. In biblical days, righteous people entered into divorce. The fact that they were forced to enter into divorce did not make them less righteous. Sometimes divorce is the best solution, but this is only because of the dehumanizing effect of sin in the world. God's ideal is always a permanent union.

If a Christian is involved in a difficult marital situation, it is incumbent upon the person to do all he or she possibly can to hold the marriage together and rebuild the relationship. Sometimes these efforts result in a genuine rebirth of marital life and the relationship is saved. Sometimes the relationship is lost.

We Christians need to remember that any sin may be forgiven by the blood of Christ. If the sinner comes to genuine repentance in his life and faith in Christ, even adultery, even murder, may be forgiven. Although there is a lack of precision in interpreting the biblical ideas regarding divorce and remarriage, there is no lack of clarity in 1 John 1:9. Persons who make a terrible mess of their marriage and bring great pain to their spouses and divorce them—these persons *too* may find forgiveness and cleansing through the blood of Christ. Such a person is likely going to have to undergo a good deal of suffering since he has been involved so deeply in a way of life which is not in harmony with God's plan (for when we violate God's laws we will bring harm to ourselves inevitably). "We cannot violate God's ideals without affecting other people—especially those closest to us. Being responsible for a divorce will not only affect the one responsible but others who are not primarily responsible. Frequently children get the worst end of the deal."[9] But forgiveness is available to all, whatever the sin, if a person is truly penitent.

In light of these conclusions, then let us seek to answer some of the most frequently raised questions in today's church. These answers are not intended to be construed as the last word; we have as yet much to learn in this area.

1. What is marriage, from a biblical viewpoint? It is the legal union of a man and woman and involves public declaration of the couple's intention to be man and wife; a committing of themselves to a permanent union; and a physical union which consummates the relationship (Gen 2:24). Mere sexual intercourse does not make a marriage. While persons may become "one flesh" they are not married unless the first two criteria are met.

2. Why is marriage so sacred a union? Marriage is a precious gift from God to be graciously received, appreciated and carefully nurtured; it is a mutual relationship between two persons and therefore can never be regarded as the sole possession or right of the one to the exclusion of the concerns of the other. Marriage is perhaps God's most wonderful means of satisfying our deepest needs for intimacy. It is God's way of bringing new human beings into the world as well. But marriage is more than all this.

Marriage is a picture to the world around of God and his love relationship to his people. This is, in the words of St. Paul, a "profound mystery." It is a mystery that a holy God should even care for a sinful people. It is a mystery that He should care enough to come and dwell among us allowing us to put him to death. It is a mystery that He should call us into union with himself and that we, by accepting his love and pledging ourselves to him, could be married to Christ. But if we accept the truth of this mystery, then we must recognize the sacredness of the marriage between a Christian man and woman, which is to be the most perfect picture here on earth of Christ's relationship with the church.

A husband's love for his wife is to be a portrayal of Christ's absolute love for us. A wife's love for her husband is to show itself in ways that demonstrate our great love for the Lord. The endurance of our love in marriage is to demonstrate his promise to love us and be with us "to the end of the age."

Christian marriage is a picture of God's commitment to us and we to him. Are we then to turn our backs on our mates and show to the world a sort of love that is indifferent and conditional? This is not the love of God, and to portray his love in this manner is to bear false witness to the world around us of the most sublime of all truths.

3. What is divorce? Divorce is a permanent breaking asunder of the marriage relationship, and involves a legal as well as personal renunciation of marriage vows and a personal cessation of cohabitation and sexual intercourse.

4. Are there any acceptable grounds for divorce for a Christian? Yes, sexual unfaithfulness and permanent desertion are mentioned by Jesus and Paul. There are other situations which might merit divorce such as extreme physical or emotional abuse to the extent that the mate's safety is endangered; or complete emotional desertion. But such grounds must be considered very seriously, and divorce taken only as a last resort. However serious the sin, the offended partner should not seek divorce unless every possible avenue toward reconciliation has been fully explored. Adultery, homosexuality, desertion, cruelty—all of these trespasses may be forgiven. There are some extreme situations, however, which are intolerable, and this is why God tolerates divorce.

5. In such circumstances, can the mate who was faithful ever be remarried? It appears that God will accept remarriage under these circumstances.

6. What about the case of two Christians who simply cannot get along together and so decide to divorce because of incompatability? We believe that any two persons who are indwelt by the Holy Spirit, if they sincerely and with true commitment seek to make a good marriage, can succeed in attaining a good marriage. Two Christians should work out their problems however demanding the cure might be. To divorce for any grounds other than those allowed by God is not acceptable, and then to go and marry someone else is doubly wrong.

7. What about the case in which one Christian partner seeks faithfully to reconcile but the other will not respond. Can a second marriage ever be justified? When there are serious difficulties in a marriage, and a spouse refuses to acknowledge the degree of the problem in marriage, other trusted Christians (a pastor, a counsellor, etc.) should be called in, and they too should confront the offender. If the spouse is still unresponsive, the partner should persist in seeking to rebuild the marriage unless or until the spouse initiates divorce. If the divorce occurs and the uncooperative partner marries again, then remarriage may occur.

8. What if a person has violated just about all God's commandments in the area of marriage and has been divorced but now has become a repentant, humble and devoted Christian—can that person ever be remarried? This is difficult. If the person has acknowledged and repented of his sin, then rather than being condemned, the person must be received and accepted as a forgiven brother or sister. Just as God forgives the premarital sins of one who repents, so God forgives post-marital sins as well.

However, before any divorced person even begins to consider remarriage, he should confront the following questions with brutal honesty:

Is there any possibility of reconciling with my former mate? Has every possible avenue to reconciliation been exhausted?

Have I demonstrated for some time now a maturity in my walk with Christ? Am I truly committed to his Lordship in my life and is my relationship to him my first priority?

Am I emotionally stable enough to be a mature marriage partner now? Chances are that the same problems which were evident in one's first marriage will arise again in a later marriage. What were they? Do my close friends feel that I have grown to the point that I will be able to be a mature, submissive Christian husband or wife? Have I really been single long enough to demonstrate that I am, on my own, psychologically and "spiritually" mature?

Am I seeking happiness in some other person because of my own personal inadequacies? Have I sought Christian counseling and been honestly satisfied that I am capable of making a mature marriage?

Is the person I am considering as a mate a divorced person also? Be very, very careful here. His or her personal problems may be compounded with your own. Only a long relationship that has proven its own degree of maturity will stand up.

NOTES

1. Gene Getz, *The Measure of a Family* (Glendale, California: Regal Books, 1976), p. 137.

2. *Parade* magazine, (Jody Foster quoted), p. 6, 11 December 1983.

3. J. Carl Laney, *The Divorce Myth* (Minneapolis: Bethany House Publishers, 1981) p. 56.

4. Bruce Metzger, *A Textual Commentary on the Greek New Testament* (London: United Bible Societies, 1971) pp. 13-14 and 47-48.

5. Laney, *Divorce Myth,* pp. 62-78, and also Guy B. Duty, *Divorce and Remarriage* (Minneapolis: Bethany House Publishers, 1967) pp. 57-62.

6. Ibid., p. 100.

7. Ibid., p. 104.

8. Laney, *Divorce Myth,* p. 87.

9. Gene Getz, *The Measure of a Family* (Glendale, California: Regal Books, 1976), p. 167.

APPENDIX C

Further Reading and Resources

THE FAMILY—GENERAL

For Me and My Family by Joyce Landorf. Vision House Publishers, Santa Ana, CA, 1977.
Seasons of a Marriage by H. Norman Wright. Regal Books, Ventura, CA, 1982.
Family Talk by Dr. Gary Collins. Vision House Publishers, Santa Ana, CA, 1978.
An Answer to Family Communication by Norman Wright. Harvest House Publishers, Irvine, CA, 1977.
The Family by Dr. John MacArthur, Jr. Moody Press, La Salle, Chicago, IL, 1982.
If I Were Starting My Family Again by John Drescher. Abingdon Press, Nashville, TN, 1979.
The Trouble with Parents edited by Tim Stafford. Zondervan, Grand Rapids, MI, 1978
What Should Parents Expect? by John M. Drescher. Abingdon, Nashville, TN, 1980.
Parents in Pain by John White. InterVarsity Press, Downer's Grove, IL, 1979.
Traits of a Healthy Family by Dolores Curran. Winston Press, Minneapolis, MN, 1983.
Prime-Time Parenting by Kay Kuzma, Ed. D., Rawson. Wade Publishers, New York, NY, 1980.

Positive Parenting by Don H. Highlander. Word, Waco, TX, 1980.
Family Communication: Keeping Connected in Changing Times by Maureen Miller. Paulist Press, New York, NY, 1980.
Parent Awareness Training: Positive Parenting for the 1980's by Saf Lerman. A & W Publishers, New York, NY, 1980.
Almost Grown: A Christian Guide for Parents of Teenagers by Dr. James R. Oraker. Harper and Row Publishers, New York, NY, 1980.
Adolescence Is Not An Illness by Bruce Narramore. Fleming H. Revell Co., Old Tappan, NJ, 1980.

DIVORCE—SINGLE PARENTING

The Single Parent by Virginia Watts. Fleming H. Revell Co., Old Tappan, NJ, 1976.
Divorced Dads by Morris A. Shepard and Gerald Goldman. Berkley Books, New York, NY, 1980.
Divorce and the Children by H.S. Vigeveno and Anne Claire. G/L Regal Books, Glendale, CA, 1979.

HUSBAND-WIFE RELATIONSHIP

Intended for Pleasure by Ed Wheat, M.D. and Gaye Wheat. Fleming H. Revell Co., Old Tappan, NJ, 1977.
Strike the Original Match by Charles R. Swindoll. Multnomah Press, Portland, OR, 1980.
Becoming One by Don Meredith. Thomas Nelson Publishers, TN, 1979.
If Only He Knew by Gary Smalley. R.M. Marketing, PA, 1979.
When You Both Go to Work by Louis and Kay More. Word Books, Waco, TX, 1982.
Discovering the Intimate Marriage (books and tape) by R. C. Sproul and Bill White. Ligonier Valley Study Center, Stahlstown, PA, 1980.
Sex Begins in the Kitchen by Dr. Kevin Leman. Regal Books, Ventura, CA, 1981.

MAGAZINES FOR KIDS

National Geographic WORLD, published by The National Geographic Society, Washington, DC.

Highlights for Children, published by Highlights for Children, Inc., Columbus, OH.

Campus Life, published monthly by Youth for Christ, Boulder, CO.

Life Notebook by the Institute in Basic Youth Conflicts, Box 1, Oak Brook, IL.

CHILDREN AND GOD

Teaching Your Child About God by Wes Haystead, Regal Books, Ventura, CA, 1974.

Breakthrough by Jay Kesler with Tim Stafford. Zondervan/Campus Life Books, Grand Rapids, MI, 1975.

FAMILY TIMES

Worldchangers, a monthly magazine published by World Literature Crusade, Studio City, CA.

The Family Devotions Idea Book by Evelyn Blitchington. Bethany House Publishers, Minneapolis, MN, 1982.

Is Anybody Listening When I Pray? by Phoebe Craner. Bethany Fellowship, Inc., Minneapolis, MN, 1980.

The Family Bible Study Book #1 and #2 edited by Betsy Scanlan. Fleming H. Revell Co., Old Tappan, NJ, 1975 and 1977.

Family Devotions with School Age Children by Lois E. LeBar. Fleming H. Revell Co., Old Tappan, NJ, 1973.

The Celebration Book edited by Georgiana Walker. Regal Books, Glendale, CA, 1979.

Good Times for Your Family by Wayne E. Rickerson. G/L Regal Books, Glendale, CA, 1976.

Four Minute Fun for Parent and Child by Elaine Hardt. Horizons, Phoenix, AZ, 1976.

"THE UNGAME," Au-Vid Inc., Garden Grove, CA.

Christian Family Activities (four separate books) by Wayne Rickerson. Standard Publishing Co., Cincinnati, OH, 1982.

Family Fun and Togetherness by Wayne Rickerson. Victor Books, Wheaton, IL, 1979.

PARENT-CHILD RELATIONSHIP

Preparing for Adolescence (book, workbook and tapes) by Dr. James Dobson. Vision House, Santa, Ana, CA.
Communication—Key to Your Teens by Norman Wright and Rex Johnson. Harvest House Publishers, Irvine, CA, 1978.
How to Really Love Your Child by Dr. Ross Campbell. Victor Books, Wheaton, IL, 1977.
The Strong-Willed Child by Dr. James Dobson. Tyndale House Publishers, Wheaton, IL, 1978.
How to Grow a Young Reader by John and Kay Lindskoog. David C. Cook Publishing Co., Elgin, IL, 1978.
God, Why Did He Die? by Anne Harler. Concordia, St. Louis, MO, 1979.
Why Did God Let Grandpa Die? by Phoebe Cranor. Dimension Books, Bethany Fellowship, Inc., Minneapolis, MN, 1976.
Heaven Has a Floor by Evelyn Roberts. The Dial Press, New York, NY, 1979.
What's Happened to Auntie Jean? by Dr. Paul White. Regal Books, Pasadena, CA, 1976.
Helping a Child Understand Death by Linda Jane Vogel. Fortress Press, Philadelphia, PA, 1975.
Tell Me About Death by Janette Klopfenstein. Herald Press, Scottsdale, PA, 1977.
The Value Tale Series by Dr. Spencer Johnson and Ann Donegan Johnson. Value Communications, Inc., San Diego, CA, 1979.
The Hurried Child by David Elkind. Addison-Wesley, Reading, MA, 1981.
Practical Parenting Tips by Vicki Lansky. Meadowbrook Books, Deep Haven, MN, 1982.

68451